FRENCH
GRAMMAR MADE EASY

A Comprehensive Workbook To Learn
French Grammar For Beginners
(Audio Included)

Lingo Mastery

ISBN: 978-1-951949-76-1

CONTENTS

PREFACE: ABOUT THE LANGUAGE
PRÉFACE: À PROPOS DE LA LANGUE FRANÇAISE

A foreign language is almost an essential communication tool for the modern era. Nowadays, French is the seventh most widely spoken language in the world, with 267 million people speaking it to varying degrees. Studies indicate that French is one of the most used languages in social networks, with 3.3 billion users.

French, a Romance language, is widely regarded as one of the most beautiful languages in the world. Today, many people think that French is no longer useful, that it is a language that is spoken less and less. Well, this is totally false! It's true that the French language no longer has the same place in the world as it did in the 19th century, but it still has a very important role and is the second most-learned language in the world after English.

French is also among the top languages for the number of countries where it has official status. It is also the only language, alongside English, that is taught in every country in the world, and it is the only language (besides English) that's spoken in all the continents (much of West Africa is French-speaking, Canada in North America, French Guinea in South America, Vanuatu in Oceania).

WHY LEARN FRENCH?
POURQUOI APPRENDRE LE FRANÇAIS ?

a. For work

Of course, nowadays, English is the main language used around the world in a work environment! But now, almost everyone speaks English, so it's no longer a "plus"; it's the minimum required. On the other hand, for your CV, knowing how to speak French is an undeniable "plus"! It will set you apart from other candidates.

b. To live and travel to France and other French speaking countries

France is the most visited country in the world! Canada is also an amazing country to explore. Even as a tourist, it is always better to know how to speak the language! Besides, the French speak very few foreign languages... So, if you want to live in France, or in a French-speaking country, there is no arguing: you will have to learn the language.

c. For your personal enrichment

Learning a language means getting to know another culture, getting to know other people and this is the best way to enrich yourself! Especially if you speak a language like French! French and France are about culture, knowledge, ideas, history, curiosity, enlightenment...

d. You will be able to speak with many more people around the world

Indeed, French is still spoken in many countries and by many people around the world: France, Canada, Belgium, Switzerland, Maghreb countries, etc. And this is increasing every day.

e. You will meet interesting and cultured people!

French is a language rich in culture. If you speak French, you will be able to access information from and about interesting people, for example on the Internet. You will also be able to communicate in everyday life with people who often have different, creative ideas.

To learn a language, it is important to have good educational resources, and books are one of the best materials—they are essential tools to achieve our goals. Finding the right resource is important, and you need the one that best suits your needs and goals. Apart from the content, the book should also be attractive and have a clear design.

This is what we are offering you with the French Grammar Workbook.

STRUCTURE
STRUCTURE

There are efficient methods that will allow you to learn French in a self-taught and independent way. These methods include complete support materials, designed to approach French in all its aspects: written and oral comprehension, and written and oral expression. A good method allows you to progress in French while having fun. The method will, ideally, simulate real-life situations. If you want to learn to communicate quickly in French, this is the book for you!

This book will introduce you to French grammar in a solid and effective way, giving you the linguistic, cultural, and strategic tools to communicate and to continue improving. This self-study tool emphasizes the practical application of formal language aspects, focusing on their real-world usage. You will learn key concepts for the use of various grammatical elements in French. This book is based on scientific research that has shown that the most effective way to remember different grammatical aspects and concepts is by stimulation and not by learning whole tables of rules by heart. In most grammar books, you will find gigantic black-and-white tables to learn by heart; this is not what you will find in this one. The purpose of this method is to stimulate and entertain you while you learn.

This book covers all aspects of French grammar while focusing on your specific needs at this point in your learning journey, specifically for someone who has an A1—A2 level. The educational progression has been carefully planned so that the student can develop experience with the use of the language, using relevant situations.

The activities have been selected to enhance communicative, linguistic, thematic, and learning domains. They include texts, cultural, and linguistic information to strengthen your knowledge of the language.

If you want to move to the next level in conversation, reading and writing while developing your grammar skills, this book is designed for you!

Of course, while "French Grammar Made Easy" can be used for self-study, it can also be used as a supplement as part of a teacher-led course.

Once you are confident with the content of this book, congratulate yourself because you will have acquired solid foundations for the rest of your learning journey. Mastering the fundamentals of French grammar is something that can take years. It is a challenge with which even native speakers can struggle their entire life.

Finally, for best results, we also advise studying the French Made Easy Level 1, the French Picture Dictionary, and French Verbs Made Easy books by Lingo Mastery.

INTRODUCTION

INTRODUCTION

The pedagogical approach adopted in the book is centered on a vision of language as a place of interaction, as a mediating dimension of the relationships established between subjects and different cultural worlds. Language does not just mean a form or system, but a set of possibilities for interaction and experience that includes not only formal structures and their rules, but also all the social, cultural, historical, and political meanings that constitute it.

Learning French means living cultural and linguistic experiences in a new language, thinking about it and the student's own mother tongue. It also means considering the student as an active subject.

This first level has the objective of developing communication and interaction skills at the initial level, in the production and reception of oral and written genres of low and medium complexity. It prepares the student to interact in French in everyday situations in different contexts.

Among the reasons to study and learn French are the possibility of communicating with French speakers in your own community, make your travel experiences more rewarding and exciting, increase your jobs prospects, improve and understand your own language better, and enjoy French music, literature, films, and theater in their original form.

RECOMMENDATIONS
RECOMMANDATIONS

The book is best for learners who have an A1+–A2 level in the Common European Framework of Reference for Languages (CEFR), which corresponds to a beginner-basic level. It is a tool for anyone who is motivated to learn French. After finishing this book, you will have a strong understanding of French at an A2+ level and will understand what you need to focus on in the next levels. Let us give you some interesting recommendations and tips:

Imposter syndrome is real when learning a foreign language, especially when learning about French grammar. Mistakes happen; everyone makes mistakes when learning a new language. Rather than discouraging us, it should encourage us to learn from our mistakes.

When learning a language, it sometimes seems difficult to remember words, but it does not mean that you have completely forgotten them, they are still somewhere in your mind. Practice will allow you to reduce the amount of time you need to remember words. This book will help you in this process by practicing as much as possible.

You do not need to rush, as each person has their own pace. Take your time; you will learn everything. And please, do not feel frustrated or disappointed if there are concepts or units that take more time than others.

Last but not least, practice makes perfect!

PRONUNCIATION GUIDE
GUIDE DE PRONONCIATION

This section is a reminder of what you should already know at an A1—A2 level. In case you are not familiar with French pronunciation or need to review some concepts, we advise reviewing the alphabet and pronunciation section of the French Made Easy Level 1 by Lingo Mastery.

ALPHABET
L'ALPHABET

UPPER-CASE	LOWER-CASE	PRONUNCIATION	IPA
A	a	*ah*	[a]
B	b	*bay*	[b]
C	c	*say*	[se]
D	d	*day*	[de]
E	e	*euh*	[ə]
F	f	*ef*	[ɛf]
G	g	*jay*	[ʒe]
H	h	*ahsh*	[aʃ]
I	i	*ee*	[i]
J	j	*jee*	[ʒi]
K	k	*kah*	[ka]
L	l	*el*	[ɛl]
M	m	*em*	[ɛm]
N	n	*en*	[ɛn]
O	o	*oh*	[o]

P	p	pay	[pe]
Q	q	koo	[ky]
R	r	air	[ɛʁ]
S	s	es	[ɛs]
T	t	tay	[te]
U	u	uh	[y]
V	v	vay	[ve]
W	w	doobleh-vay	[dublǝve]
X	x	eeks	[iks]
Y	y	ee-grec	[i gʁɛk]
Z	z	zed	[zɛd]

VOWELS
LES VOYELLES

A	→	sounds like *ah*	→	as in c**a**t, *father*
E/EU	→	sounds like *euh*	→	as in f**u**r, *pl**eu**voir* (to rain)
É	→	sounds like *hey*	→	as in *caf**é**, t**é**léviseur* (television)
È/Ê	→	sounds like *bet*	→	as in *p**ai**r, **ai**r* (air)
I/Y	→	sounds like *ee*	→	as in f**ee**t, *diff**i**c**i**le* (difficult)
O/AU/EAU	→	sounds like *oh*	→	as in P**o**land, *gât**eau*** (cake)
OI	→	sounds like *wah*	→	as in s**wa**n, *p**oi**re* (pear)
U	→	sounds like *u*	→	as in t**u**t**u**, *ü**ber*
OU	→	sounds like *oo*	→	as in f**oo**l, *p**ou**le* (hen)

CONSONANTS
LES CONSONNES

C + E/I/Ç	→	sounds like *ss*	→	as in **c**enter, i**c**i (here), **ç**a va ? (how are you?)
C + other letters	→	sounds like *kah*	→	as in **c**atastrophe, **c**ombien (how much)
CH	→	sounds like *sh*	→	as in **sh**ell, mar**ch**e (work/walks)
G + E/I	→	sounds like *je*	→	as in gara**ge**, **g**île (cottage)
G + other letters	→	sounds like *geh*	→	as in **gr**ass, **gr**ammaire (grammar)
GN	→	sounds like *nyeh*	→	as in onion, campa**gn**e (countryside)
H	→	is *silent!*	→	as in **h**eir, **h**ôtel (hotel)
QU	→	sounds like *keh*	→	as in **qu**estion, **qu**iche
LL	→	sounds like *elle*	→	as in be**ll**e (beautiful), vi**ll**e (city)
LL	→	sounds like *yeh*	→	as in fi**ll**e (girl), je travai**ll**e (I work)

A FEW MORE RULES

In French, you pronounce **j, b, d, p, t** more softly than in English, while the letter **r** is rolled a lot more. In French, the consonants C, R, F, and L are often pronounced at the end of words, as remembered by the acronym CaReFuL. Examples include 'par**c**' (park, pronounced 'park'), 'au **r**evoir' (goodbye, pronounced 'oh reh-vwar'), 'soi**f**' (thirst, pronounced 'swahf'), and 'Noë**l**' (Christmas, pronounced 'no-el').

When a word ends in an **s** and is followed by a vowel, you can link both sounds together. This is called a *liaison*: Ils ont des chats adorables, They have adorable cats = ils_**z**_ont des chats adorables.

INTRODUCTION TO FRENCH GRAMMAR
INTRODUCTION À LA GRAMMAIRE FRANÇAISE

A language can almost be considered as a form of art. It provides you with tools and concepts that you can use in whichever way you wish to convey meaning, intention, emotions, and many more other things.

Linguistics is divided into the following subfields:

a. **phonetics**: the study of human speech sounds,

b. **phonology**: the study of the use of human speech,

c. **morphology**: the study of internal structures of morphemes, and which is a subfield of grammar,

d. **lexicology**: the study of words and the relations between them,

e. **orthographic linguistics**: the study of orthography,

f. **syntax**: the study of rules for constructing sentences in a language,

g. **semantics**: the study of meaning in a language,

h. and finally, **pragmatics**: the study of language from the users' viewpoint, how words are used in context, how their meanings differ based on who is speaking, etc.

Now, you may be wondering, what does this all have to do with **grammar**? Grammar is the field that studies the set of **structural rules and constraints** applied in the formation of **clauses** (at least a noun and a verb), **phrases** (parts of speech, e.g., noun, adjectival, or adverbial phrases), and **words** (single units of language). The study of grammar includes fields such as **morphology** and **syntax**.

Do you recognize the words "**morphology**" and "**syntax**"? Yes, they are in the list above, c and f respectively. Several of the fields mentioned in the list above are part of the study of grammar.

HOW TO GET THE AUDIO FILES

Some of the exercises throughout this book come with accompanying audio files.
You can download these audio files if you head over to:
www.lingomastery.com/french-gme-audio

If you're having trouble downloading the audio, contact us at
www.lingomastery.com/contact

THE VERB TO BE
LE VERBE ÊTRE

Welcome to the first unit of French Grammar Made Easy by Lingo Mastery. The purpose of this workbook, as explained in the introductory chapters, is for you to learn key concepts of French grammar, which means we will not cover conjugation per se, the purpose of "French Verbs Made Easy" by Lingo Mastery. In this workbook, we will focus on all concepts from a purely grammatical perspective, including when it comes to verbs. Therefore, we assume you already understand the basics of French conjugation that corresponds to the A1+–A2+ (upper lower beginner and upper higher beginner) levels within the CEFR Framework.

A PILLAR
UN PILIER

The verb **être** (*to be*) is one of the most useful verbs in dialogues.

> **a.** Je **suis** heureux.
> *I am happy.*

> **b.** Vous **êtes** norvégiens.
> *You (pl.) are Norwegian.*

> Note : Vous" is used for formal situations or when addressing multiple people, while "tu" is used for informal situations with friends, family, or people of the same ag*e group.*

> **c.** D'où **êtes**-vous ?
> *Where **are** you from?*

The verb **être** is very useful if you want to tell people where you are from. *D'où êtes-vous ?* means *where are you from?*

Some example sentences to tell where you are from:

> **a.** Je **suis** de Berlin.
> *I am from Berlin.*

> **b.** Tu **es** de New York.
> *You are from New York.*

> **c.** Il **est** de Lima.
> *He is from Lima.*

If the word following **de** starts with a vowel, **de** becomes **d'**.

For example:

    a. Je **suis d'**Angers.
       I am from Angers.

For example:

    b. Je **suis d'**Amiens.
       I am from Amiens.

AT, FROM
À, DE, CHEZ

You just learned how to use **être + de**; you can also use **être + à** to indicate in which city you are currently in.

For example:

    a. Je **suis à** Lyon.
       I am in Lyon.

    b. Nous **sommes à** Dehli.
       We are in Dehli.

    c. Ils **sont à** Montréal.
       They are in Montreal.

You can also use **être + chez** when you are at someone's house.

For example:

    a. Je **suis chez** Luc.
       I am at Luc's.

    b. Vous **êtes chez** des amis.
       You are at some friends' house

EXERCISES
EXERCICES

1. Fill in the gaps. *Remplissez les trous.*

    a. Ils _____ d'où ?
    Where are they from?

    b. _____ suis allemand. Je _____ de Berlin.
    I am German. I am from Berlin.

    c. Et toi, tu _____ d'où ?
    And you, where are you from?

    d. _____ suis de Sofia. _____ _____ bulgare.
    I am from Sofia. I am Bulgarian.

    e. Vous _____ d'où ? _____ sommes de Pékin. Nous _____ chinois.
    Where are you (pl.) from? We are from Beijing. We are Chinese.

    f. Elle _____ d'où ? Elle _____ du Paraguay.
    Where is she from? She is from Paraguay.

    g. Tu _____ marié ?
    Are you married?

    h. Non, je _____ célibataire.
    No, I am single.

    i. Et vous, _____ _____ mariés ?
    And you (pl.), are you married?

    j. Oui, _____ _____ mariés.
    Yes, we are married.

2. **Answer the questions with the reply of your choice, like in the example**. *Répondez aux questions avec la réponse de votre choix tel que dans l'exemple.*

Vous êtes français ou suisse ? *Are you French or Swiss?*

Je suis suisse. *I am Swiss.*

a. Vous êtes mariée ou célibataire ? *Are you married or single?*

_____

b. Vous êtes scientifique ou artiste ? *Are you a scientist or an artist?*

_____

c. Vous êtes parisienne ou bordelaise ? *Are you Parisian or from Bordeaux?*

_____

d. Vous êtes d'Italie ou du Vietnam ? *Are you from Italy or Vietnam?*

_____

e. Vous êtes de Malaisie ou d'Argentine ? *Are you from Malaysia or from Argentina?*

_____

3. **Introduce the people as shown in the example**. *Présentez les personnes comme dans l'exemple.*

LETTER	NAME	NATIONALITY	CITY OF ORIGIN	CURRENT ADDRESS
a	Magdalena	polonaise / Polish	Varsovie / Warsaw	Hôtel Stonehenge / Stonehenge Hotel
b	Chiara	italienne / Italian	Livourne / Livorno	Chez un ami à Pékin / At a friend's in Beijing
c	Hao Dong	chinois / Chinese	Dandong / Dandong	Hôtel Aspen à New York / Aspen Hotel in New York
d	Viktoriya	bulgare / Bulgarian	Sofia / Sofia	Chez mes cousins à Oslo / At my cousins' in Oslo
e	Paulo	brésilien / Brazilian	Sao Paulo / Sao Paulo	Dans ma maison de vacances à Marrakech / In my holiday house in Marrakech
f	Steve	anglais / English	Newcastle / Newcastle	Au camping Les Hirondelles / At the Campsite Les Hirondelles

Example:

a. Je m'appelle Magdalena. Je suis polonaise. Je suis de Varsovie. Je suis à l'hôtel Stonehenge, à Londres.

My name is Magdalena. I am Polish. I am from Warsaw. I am at the Hotel Stonehenge in London.

b. _____

_____

c. _____

_____

d. _____

_____

e. _____

_____

f. _____

_____

ADJECTIVES
LES ADJECTIFS

MASCULINE AND FEMININE FORMS OF ADJECTIVES IN FRENCH
MASCULIN ET FÉMININ DES ADJECTIFS FRANÇAIS

As a general rule, to form the feminine form of adjectives, adding an **-e** to the masculine form is sufficient.

For example:

a. Masculine: Michel est petit.
Michel is short.

b. Feminine: Micheline est petit**e**.
Micheline is short.

Second example:

a. Masculine: Frédéric est fort.
Frédéric is strong.

b. Feminine: Frédérique est fort**e**.
Frédérique is strong.

Same forms for both the masculine and the feminine

If the masculine form already ends with an **-e**, then the feminine form is the same as the masculine form.

For example:

a. Masculine: Pierre est dynami**que**.
Pierre is energetic.

b. Feminine: Pierrette est dynami**que**.
Pierrette is energetic.

Adjectives that end with a consonant

When an adjective ends with a consonant, such as -**s**, -**d** or -**t**, that consonant is silent, but it becomes audible when in the feminine form because of the added -**e** ending.

For example:

    a. Masculine: Il est grand.
       He is tall.

    b. Feminine: Elle est grand**e**.
       She is tall.

Second example:

    a. Masculine: Le ciel est gris.
       The sky is gray.

    b. Feminine: La souris est gris**e**.
       The mouse is gray.

Doubled consonant

Sometimes, the last consonant is **doubled** in the feminine form.

For example:

    a. Masculine: Le plat est bon.
       The dish is good.

    b. Feminine: La soupe est bon**ne**.
       The soup is good.

    c. Masculine: Le chat est gros.
       The cat is big.

    d. Feminine: La chatte est gros**se**.
       The female cat is big.

There is no fixed rule to know when the last consonant is doubled in the feminine form or not, but usually adjectives that end in **-el**, **-eil**, **-ien**, **-on**, **-et,** or **-s** have their ending doubled in the feminine form.

For example:

  a. Masculine: Un voyage officiel.
  An official trip.

  b. Feminine: Une déclaration officie**ll**e.
  An official statement.

Complete change of ending

Sometimes, the ending has to change completely. There are many exceptions in French, but the following rules can usually be applied:

  a. Adjectives that end in **-f** in the masculine form end in **-ve** in the feminine form

  b. **-x** in the masculine form usually turns into **-se** in the feminine form

  c. -**eur** usually turns into -**euse** or **-ice**

  d. **-er** usually turns into -**ère**

For example:

  a. Masculine: Il est paresseu**x**.
  He is lazy.

  b. Feminine: Elle est paresseu**se**.
  She is lazy.

  c. Masculine: Il est sporti**f**.
  He is athletic.

  d. Feminine: Elle est sporti**ve**.
  She is athletic.

  e. Masculine: Il est serv**eur**.
  He is a waiter.

  f. Feminine: Elle est serv**euse**.
  She is a waitress.

  g. Masculine: Il est act**eur**.
  He is an actor.

  h. Feminine: Elle est actr**ice**.
  She is an actress.

  i. Masculine: Il est fi**er**.
  He is proud.

  j. Feminine: Elle est fi**ère**.
  She is proud.

SINGULAR AND PLURAL OF ADJECTIVES IN FRENCH
SINGULIER ET PLURIEL DES ADJECTIFS EN FRANÇAIS

Mixed groups / Groupes mixtes

When forming the plural in French, if the subject is *composed of both feminine and masculine* forms, the *adjective agrees with the masculine plural form*.

For example:

a. Plural: Laurent et Laura sont grand**s**.
Laurent and Laura are tall.

The general rule in French to build the plural form of an adjective is to add an **-s** to its ending.

For example:

a. Singular: Le scientifique est intéressant.
The scientist is interesting.

b. Plural: Les scientifiques sont intéressant**s**.
The scientists are interesting.

Second example:

a. Singular: L'enfant est petit.
The child is short.

b. Plural: Les enfants sont petit**s**.
The children are short.

To form the feminine plural form, follow the rules you learned in the previous section of this unit to form the feminine form, and add an -**s** to the ending.

For example:

    a. Singular: Yvette est grande.
      Yvette is tall.

    b. Plural: Yvette et Colette sont grande**s**.
      Yvette and Colette are tall.

-s and -x endings / Terminaisons en -s et en -x

When an adjective ends with an -**s** or an -**x**, the ending in the plural form remains the same.

For example:

    a. Singular: Il est japonais.
      He is Japanese.

    b. Plural: Ils sont japonais.
      They are Japanese.

    c. Singular: Il est audacieux.
      He is daring.

    d. Plural: Ils sont audacieux.
      They are daring.

As you saw in the previous section of this unit, -**x** generally turns into -**se** in the feminine form, so the feminine plural form is built by using the feminine form and adding an -**s** to it.

For example:

    a. Singular: Elle est audacieu**se**.
      She is daring.

    b. Plural: Elles sont audacieu**ses**.
      They (fem. pl.) are daring.

-al and -au endings / Terminaisons en -al et en -au

-al and -au usually turn into -aux in the plural.

For example:

   a. Singular: Le tableau est original.
   The painting is original.

   b. Plural: Les tableaux sont originaux.
   The paintings are original.

   c. Singular: Le paysage est beau.
   The landscape is beautiful.

   d. Plural: Les paysages sont beaux.
   The landscapes are beautiful.

There are some exceptions, such as **banals**.

For example:

   a. Singular: Un livre banal.
   An unremarkable book.

   b. Plural: Des livres banals.
   Unremarkable books.

The feminine plural form of -al is -ales.

For example:

   a. Singular: Elle est originale.
   She is original.

   b. Plural: Elles sont originales.
   They (fem. pl.) are originals.

Color adjectives / Adjectifs de couleur

Color adjectives agree with the noun they modify in both singular and plural forms. However, when the color adjective is derived from a thing (like a fruit or an object), it remains invariable.

For example, **orange** means **orange** as the **color,** but also means **orange** as in the **fruit**. Therefore:

    a. Singular: Une feuille orang**e**.
    An orange leaf.

    b. Plural: Des feuilles orang**e**.
    Orange leaves.

The same applies to **marron,** which means **brown,** as in the **color** of **chestnut**. There are exceptions though. The only one you need to remember at your current level is **rose,** which means **pink**. The adjective *rose agrees with the subject.*

For example:

    a. Singular: Un cahier ros**e**.
    A pink notebook.

    b. Plural: Des cahiers ros**es**.
    Pink notebooks.

    c. Singular: Un pull marron.
    A brown sweater.

    d. Plural: Des pulls marron.
    Brown sweaters.

Compound adjectives also *remain invariable* in their plural form.

 **EXERCISES**
EXERCICES

1. Put the adjectives in the feminine form like in the example. *Mettez les adjectifs au féminin comme dans l'exemple.*

For example:

Jack est allemand.
Jack is German.

Mary est allemande.
Mary is German.

    a. Monsieur Martin est sympathique.
    Mr. Martin is friendly.

        Madame Martin est _____.
        Mrs. Martin is friendly.

    b. Mon oncle est intelligent.
    My uncle is intelligent.

        Ma tante est _____.
        My aunt is intelligent.

    c. Mon frère est blond.
    My brother is blond.

        Ma sœur est _____.
        My sister is blond.

    d. Le garçon est souriant.
    The boy is cheerful.

        La fille est _____.
        The girl is cheerful.

e. Mon père est créatif.
My father is creative.

Ma mère est _____.
My mother is creative.

2. Listen to the sentences and fill in the gaps with the adjectives in their correct form. *Écoutez et remplissez les trous avec les adjectifs dans leur forme correcte. (Find audio on page 12.)*

a. Stéphane et Henri sont _____.
Stéphane and Henri are jealous.

b. Les cousins de Matthieu sont _____.
Matthieu's cousins have brown hair.

c. Les fleurs sont _____.
The flowers are pink.

d. Les tasse (feminine word) sont _____.
The cups are colored.

e. Les contes (masculine word) sont _____.
The tales are original.

3. Write the adjective in the feminine or masculine form like in the example. *Mettez l'adjectif au féminin ou au masculin comme dans l'exemple.*

Example:

M. Martin est **grand et intelligent**.
Mr. Martin is tall and intelligent.

Mme Martin est **grande et intelligente**.
Mrs. Martin is tall and intelligent.

a. La mère de Jean-Claude est _____ et _____ .
Jean-Claude's mother is blond and short.

b. Le père de Jean Claude est est _____ et _____ .
Jean-Claude's father is blond and short.

c. L'infirmier est _____ et _____ .
The male nurse is kind and professional.

d. L'infirmière est _____ et _____ .
The female nurse is kind and professional.

e. Lucie est _____ et _____ .
Lucie is pretty and sympathetic.

f. Michel est _____ et _____ .
Michel is handsome and sympathetic.

g. L'enseignant est _____ et _____ .
The male teacher is tanned and muscular.

h. L'enseignante est _____ et _____ .
The female teacher is tanned and muscular.

NEGATION AND INTERROGATION
NÉGATION ET INTERROGATION

SIMPLE NEGATION
NÉGATION SIMPLE

In French, **simple negation** is built as such:

a. **ne** + verb + **pas**

For example:

a. Je **ne** mange **pas**.
I do not eat.

Ne turns into **n'** when followed by a vowel:

a. Vous **n'**êtes pas fatigués.
You are not tired.

SIMPLE QUESTION
QUESTION SIMPLE

A simple question is a question that accepts *yes or no as an answer*.

Orally, a simple sentence can be turned into a simple question with a rising tone at the end of the sentence:

    a. Vous êtes français ?
       Lit. You are French? Meaning: Are you French?

A simple question can also be used as such:

    Est-ce que + sentence ?

For example:

    a. Est-ce que Jeanine est malade ?
       Is Jeanine sick?

    b. Est-ce que tu manges du fromage ?
       Do you eat cheese?

Another way to build simple questions is to invert the verb and the subject. When the subject is a personal pronoun (*je, tu, il/elle/on*, etc.), this is straightforward:

    a. Sentence: **Vous êtes** canadien.
       You are Canadian.

    b. Simple question: **Êtes-vous** canadien ?
       Are you (sing. form.) Canadian?

When the subject is not a pronoun, a *pronoun can be added* to the sentence to build a simple question. The pronoun must be the right one for the subject.

    a. Sentence: Michael **est** écossais.
       Michael is Scottish.

b. Simple question: Michael **est-il** écossais ?
Is Michael Scottish?

In this example, we use **il** because Michael is a masculine subject.

ANSWERING SIMPLE QUESTIONS
RÉPONDRE À DES QUESTIONS SIMPLES

Oui, which means *yes* is used in a similar way as in English. It is used in affirmative answers:

a. Question: Est-ce que tu as faim ?
Are you hungry?

b. Answer: **Oui**, j'ai faim.
Yes, I am hungry.

Non, which means *no,* negates the entire sentence.

a. Question: Tu travailles aujourd'hui ?
Are you working today?

b. Answer: **Non**.
No.

Si, which has no English equivalent, is used to contradict a negative sentence or question:

a. Negative sentence: Le chien **ne** mord **pas**.
The dog does not bite.

a. Answer: **Si**, il mord.
Yes, it does.

b. Negative question: Vous **ne** vivez **pas** en France ?
You do not live in France?

b. Answer: **Si**, nous vivons en France.
Yes, we do.

Pas denies a part of the question:

  a. Question: Tu n'aimes pas les œufs ?
  You do not like eggs?

  b. Answer: **Pas** au petit-déjeuner.
  Not for breakfast.

Finally, **moi non plus** is used to confirm a negation.

  a. Negative sentence: Je **ne** mange **pas** de poires.
  I do not eat pears.

  b. Answer: **Moi non plus**.
  Neither do I.

EXERCISES
EXERCICES

1. **Put the affirmative sentences in the negative form like in the example**. *Mettez les phrases affirmatives à la forme négative comme dans l'exemple.*

Affirmative: Ma mère travaille le samedi.
My mother works on Saturdays.

Negative: Ma mère **ne** travaille **pas** le samedi.
My mother does not work on Saturdays.

   a. Affirmative: La porte est fermée.
      The door is shut.

      Negative: _____.
      The door is not shut.

   b. Affirmative: Je suis du Pérou.
      I am from Peru.

      Negative: _____.
      I am not from Peru.

   c. Affirmative: La salade est bonne.
      The salad is good.

      Negative: _____.
      The salad is not good.

   d. Affirmative: Ils ont plusieurs ordinateurs.
      They have several computers.

      Negative: _____.
      They do not have several computers.

   e. Affirmative: Ceci est un masque.
      This is a mask.

      Negative: _____.
      This is not a mask.

2. Answer with "moi aussi" or "moi non plus" like in the example. *Répondez avec moi aussi ou moi non plus comme dans l'exemple.*

    a. J'aime les mathématiques.
       I like mathematics.

    Moi aussi.

    b. Je n'aime pas la musique.
       I do not like music.

    _____

    c. Je ne suis pas fatigué.
       I am not tired.

    _____

    d. Je suis belge.
       I am Belgian.

    _____

    e. Je ne suis pas à Londres.
       I am not in London.

    _____

    f. Je travaille dans une grande entreprise.
       I work in a big company.

    _____

NOUNS AND ARTICLES
NOMS ET ARTICLES

In this section, we are going to cover quite a few points. Unlike English, French **nouns** are always **masculine** or **feminine**. Besides, nouns are usually preceded by a **definite** (equivalent of *the* in English) or an **indefinite** (equivalent of *a/an* in English) article.

For example:

a. **La** saucisse.
The sausage.

b. **Le** pain.
The bread.

c. **La** Suisse.
Switzerland.

d. **Le** Japon.
Japan.

e. **Un** pays.
A country.

f. **Un** plat.
A dish.

g. **Un** ordinateur.
A computer.

h. **Une** tasse.
A cup.

MASCULINE AND FEMININE
MASCULIN ET FÉMININ

Nouns that refer to people

When talking about people in French, the grammatical gender aligns with their **gender**.

For example:

a. Masculine: **un** client
a male customer

b. Feminine: **une** cliente
a female customer

As a general rule, one usually adds an **-e** to the end of the masculine form to build the feminine form, which is similar to what you learned in the section about adjectives.

For example:

    a. Masculine: **un** client brun
       a brown-haired customer

    b. Feminine: **une** cliente brune
       a brown-haired female customer

When a noun ends with an **-e**, one changes only the article to build the feminine form. Nouns that remain the same in both the masculine and feminine forms are called *epicenes*. In French, those nouns are considered as gender-neutral; but they are not completely gender-neutral, as it is understood in English, since the article changes, too (**le** or **la**, **un** or **une**).

For example:

    a. Masculine: **un** architecte
       a male architect

    b. Feminine: **une** architecte
       a female architect

Sometimes, the ending changes completely.

For example:

    a. Masculine: **un** coiffeur
       a male hairdresser

    b. Feminine: **une** coiffeuse
       a female hairdresser

As a general rule, you can remember the following rules to build the feminine forms from the masculine ones:

    a. the ending **-en** turns into **-enne**

    b. the ending **-on** turns into **-onne**

    c. the ending **-eur** turns into **-euse**

    d. the ending **-teur** turns into **-trice**

As usual in French, there are also exceptions, sometimes **-teur** turns into **-teuse** in the feminine form, <u>for example:</u>

    a. Masculine: **un** chanteur
        a male singer

    b. Feminine: **une** chanteuse
        a female singer

But:

    a. Masculine: **un** instituteur
        a male primary school teacher

    b. Feminine: **une** institutrice
        a female primary school teacher

There are many more exceptions, including cases where the masculine and feminine forms are completely different words. Covering all of them is beyond the scope of this book. However, here are some of the <u>most common examples:</u>

    a. Masculine: **un** garçon
        a boy

    b. Feminine: **une** fille
        a girl

Second example:

    a. Masculine: **un** homme
        a man

    b. Feminine: **une** femme
        a woman

EXERCISES
EXERCICES

1. Listen to each sentence as it is read in the masculine form. Then, write the sentences in the feminine form. *Écoutez chaque phrase telle qu'elle est lue au masculin. Ensuite, écrivez les phrases au féminin. (Find audio on page 12.)*

a. Un chat noir boit du lait.
A black cat is drinking milk.

_____

b. Le chien de ma grand-mère est grand.
My grandmother's dog is big.

_____

c. Le chanteur grec est brun.
The Greek singer has brown hair.

_____

d. Mon mari est fort et sympathique.
My husband is strong and friendly.

_____

e. C'est un acteur français connu.
It is a famous French actor.

_____

f. Le voisin chinois est sympathique et créatif.
The Chinese neighbor is friendly and creative.

_____

TALKING ABOUT THINGS
PARLER DE CHOSES

When talking about objects, *there is no such thing as gender or sex*. Therefore, one cannot guess whether a table or a fruit will be **feminine** or **masculine**.

Ideally, *you should always learn the article along with its noun*. For example, if you want to say you ate an apple yesterday and you do not know how to say apple, you will probably look it up in the dictionary and discover that apple in French is **pomme**. Instead of just learning **pomme**, you should learn its articles, too: **une pomme** or **la pomme**.

Note that in the dictionary it is usually not written **le/la or un/une,** but rather **nf** or **nm**.

- **nm** means **nom masculin** and means that the noun is **masculine**.

- **nf** means **nom féminin** and means that the noun is **feminine**.

Of course, we are well aware that learning every new noun with its articles is not always possible, especially if you learn new words by hearing them in a conversation or if you ask someone how to say something. Luckily, there are a few mnemonics to remember whether nouns are masculine or feminine. They are not general rules, but they work in most cases.

a. Masculine Endings

-age: un avant**age** (an advantage), un gar**age** (a garage)

-eau: un chât**eau** (a castle), un tabl**eau** (a painting)

-isme: un optim**isme** (an optimism), un réal**isme** (a realism)

-ment: un mo**ment** (a moment), un apparte**ment** (an apartment)

-phone: un télé**phone** (a telephone), un xylo**phone** (a xylophone)

-scope: un micro**scope** (a microscope), un télescope (a telescope)

b. Feminine endings:

-ade: une limon**ade** (a lemonade), une promen**ade** (a walk)

-ance: une ch**ance** (a chance), une import**ance** (an importance)

-ence: une différ**ence** (a difference), une expéri**ence** (an experience)

-ette: une fourch**ette** (a fork), une cass**ette** (a cassette tape)

-ode: une méth**ode** (a method), une péri**ode** (a period)

-sion: une déci**sion** (a decision), une télévi**sion** (a television)

-té: une beau**té** (a beauty), une liber**té** (a freedom)

-tion: une na**tion** (a nation), une conversa**tion** (a conversation)

-ude: une atti**tude** (an attitude), une habi**tude** (a habit)

Now, apart from those in this list of feminine endings, many nouns that end with **-e** are usually **masculine,** nouns such as **un problème** (*a problem*), **un répertoire** (*a notebook*), or **un programme** (*a program*).

Finally, some nouns that end in **-eur** can be feminine, such as **une fleur** (*a flower*) or **une erreur** (*a mistake*).

TALKING ABOUT ANIMALS
PARLER DES ANIMAUX

In the previous section, we were talking about things; but what about nouns that refer to **animals**? Some animals can be referred to using **two nouns,** depending on their **sex.**

For example:

    a. Masculine: **le** coq
       the rooster

    b. Feminine: **la** poule
       the hen

Second example:

    a. Masculine: **le** chien
       the dog

    b. Feminine: **la** chienne
       the female dog

EXERCISES
EXERCICES

2. **Fill in the gaps with either "le" or "la".** *Remplissez les trous avec "le" ou "la".*

   a. _____ fromage suisse fondant, c'est ça _____ solution !
   A Swiss cheese that melts, that is the solution!

   b. Quand _____ téléphone sonne, j'éteins _____ télévision.
   When the phone rings, I turn off the television.

   c. _____ salade est très bonne. _____ nourriture de ce restaurant est excellente.
   The salad is delicious. That restaurant's food is excellent.

   d. _____ méthode d'apprentissage est intéressante.
   The learning method is interesting.

   e. Mon style littéraire préféré, c'est _____ réalisme.
   My favorite literary style is realism.

3. **Fill in the gaps with "un" or "une".** *Remplissez les trous avec "un" ou "une".*

   a. _____ garçon va à l'école.
   A boy goes to school.

   b. _____ téléscope est un instrument scientifique pour les astronomes.
   A telescope is a scientific instrument for astronomers.

   c. _____ culture agricole est visible depuis l'espace.
   An agricultural culture is visible from space.

   d. _____ différence existe entre les deux écoles.
   There is a difference between the two schools.

   e. _____ peur incontrôlable n'aide jamais.
   An uncontrollable fear never helps.

f. _____ programme intéressant vient d'être publié récemment.
An interesting programme was recently published.

g. _____ assiette verte se trouve dans la pile d'assiettes rouges.
A green plate is in the stack of red plates.

h. _____ chat jeune et joueur ne convient pas à une personne âgée.
A young and playful cat is not convenient for an old person.

i. _____ page blanche est apparue dans le document.
A blank page appeared in the document.

j. _____ âge intéressant pour une tortue.
An interesting age for a turtle.

k. _____ cage est sur le toit de ma voiture.
A cage is on the roof of my car.

SINGULAR AND PLURAL OF NOUNS
NOMS SINGULIERS ET PLURIELS

In French, the general rule is that an **-s** is usually added at the end of a noun to *form the plural*.

For example:

    a. Singular: une cage
       a cage

    b. Plural: des cage**s**
       cages

However, when a noun ends with **-s**, **-x,** or **-z,** the plural form remains **identical** to the singular form.

For example:

    a. Singular: une croix
       a cross

    b. Plural: des croix
       crosses

Second example:

    a. Singular: un cas
       a case

    b. Plural: des cas
       cases

Third example:

    a. Singular: un gaz
       a gas

    b. Plural: des gaz
       gases

Then, most words that end in **-al**, **-au** or **-eau** have their plural form built by replacing those endings with **-aux**.

For example:

    a. Singular: un chev**al**
       a horse

    b. Plural: des chev**aux**
       horses

Second example:

    a. Singular: un tuy**au**
       a pipe

    b. Plural: des tuy**aux**
       pipes

Third example:

    a. Singular: un cham**eau**
       a camel

    b. Plural: des cham**eaux**
       camels

Moreover, usually, nouns that end in **-ail** have a regular ending:

    a. Singular: un détail
       a detail

    b. Plural: des détail**s**
       details

However, there are exceptions.

For example:

    a. Singular: un trav**ail**
    a job

    b. Plural: des trav**aux**
    jobs

This one is one of the simpler examples and there are more that we will not cover in the scope of this book as they are more complex.

The ending **-eu** becomes **-eux** in the plural form.

For example:

    a. Singular: un cheveu
    one hair

    b. Plural: deux cheveu**x**
    two hairs

Second example:

    a. Singular: un jeu
    a game

    b. Plural: deux jeu**x**
    two games

To form the plural of nouns that end in **-ou**, there is no rule. In their plural form, they either end in **-ous** or in **-oux**.

For example:

    a. Singular: un genou
    a knee

    b. Plural: deux genou**x**
    two knees

But:

a. Singular: un bisou
a kiss

b. Plural: deux bisou**s**
two kisses

And as usual, there are some more exceptions in French. The best is to learn examples as you encounter them and enrich your vocabulary. One example of a <u>common noun</u>:

a. Singular: un **œil**
an eye

b. Plural: des **yeux**
eyes

Second example with another common noun:

a. Singular: un œuf
an egg

b. Plural: des œufs
eggs

Note: in its **singular** form, the **f** at the end of **œuf** is pronounced. In its plural form **œufs**, the ending **fs** is **silent**.

 **EXERCISES**
EXERCICES

1. **Rewrite the text with all the bold nouns and adjectives in their plural form**. *Réécrivez le texte avec tous les noms et adjectifs en gras au pluriel.*

Ce matin, je me suis levé et j'ai bu **un café allongé** (_____).

J'ai mangé **un croissant** (_____), **une fraise mûre**

(_____.) et **une orange sanguine** (_____.).

Ensuite, j'ai vu **un vélo** (_____.) devant ma maison. Mon voisin a **une amie**

américaine (_____). D'habitude, ses amis américains lui ramènent **un**

ordinateur (_____.) des États-Unis.

J'ai **un fils** (_____.) et **une fille** (_____.). Je les ai emmenés à l'école

à 8h30. Ils ont **un instituteur** (_____.) et deux institutrices qui sont très

sympathiques.

En cours de sport, le professeur a donné **une balle** (_____.) aux élèves.

Ils se sont beaucoup amusés.

Le soir, **le chat** (_____.) du voisin est venu dans notre maison. Il joue avec

le chien (_____.) du voisin, parfois. Ils sont très mignons.

Translation of the text

This morning, I woke up and I drank an americano. I ate a croissant, a ripe strawberry, and a red orange. Then I saw a bicycle in front of my house. My neighbor has an American female friend. Usually, his American friends bring him a computer from the United States.

I have a son and a daughter. I brought them to school at 8:30. They have a male and two female teachers who are very friendly.

In physical education class, the professor gave a ball to the students. They had a lot of fun.

In the evening, the neighbor's cat came to our house. It plays with the neighbor's dog sometimes. They are very cute.

2. Write the nominal groups in the plural form like in the example. *Mettez les groupes nominaux au pluriel comme dans l'exemple.*

Example:

Un jus d'orange / *An orange juice*

Des jus d'orange / Orange juices

   a. Un œil vert / *A green eye*

   b. Un cheveu marron / *A brown hair*

   c. Un chat blanc / *A white cat*

   d. Un animal de compagnie / *A pet*

   e. Un bijou magnifique / *A magnificent jewel*

   f. Un pneu crevé / *A flat tire*

   g. Un cheval merveilleux / *A wonderful horse*

ARTICLES
ARTICLES

In this chapter, you are going to review basic concepts about articles and deepen your knowledge about them. As a reminder, articles in French are either **masculine** or **feminine**, **singular**, or **plural** and **finite** or **indefinite**.

INDEFINITE ARTICLE
ARTICLES INDÉFINIS

An **indefinite article** can refer to a **category** of **people** or **things** in opposition to a specific one.

For example:

    a. Un chat
      A cat

In this example, you can see that we do not know which cat we are talking about. In a sentence, it can be used <u>this way</u>:

    b. J'ai vu un chat dans le village.
      I saw a cat in the village.

We know that there is **a** cat in the village, but *we do not know which one.*

The feminine form of **un** is **une**.

For example:

    c. J'ai vu **une** souris dans la ville.
      I saw a mouse in the city.

Once again, we do not know which mouse we are talking about.

Un or **une** can also refer to the counting unit **one** (**1**).

For example:

> **d.** J'ai **un** chien, pas deux.
> *I have one dog, not two.*

Also, do not forget about the **liaisons** in French. When a masculine noun starts with a **vowel**, the n in **un** is **not silent** anymore: **un avocat** / *an avocado or a lawyer* (pronunciation: un **n**avoka).

DEFINITE ARTICLES
ARTICLES DÉFINIS

A **definite** article, as opposed to an indefinite article, refers to **something** or **someone specific**. If we take our previous example:

> **a.** J'ai vu le chat dans le village.
> *I saw the cat in the village.*

In this sentence, we are talking about a **specific** cat. Without context, we understand that there is **one only cat** in the village and the speaker has seen that one cat in particular.

The feminine form of **le** is **la**.

For example:

> **b.** J'ai vu la souris dans le laboratoire.
> *I saw the mouse in the laboratory.*

The definite articles **le** and **la** can also be used to refer to general concepts; here are a few examples:

a. La grammaire française
French grammar

c. La politique
Politics

b. La liberté d'expression
Freedom of speech

d. Le bonheur
Happiness

Language and meaning often depend on the context. For example, consider the following sentence:

a. J'aime le pain.

This sentence can either mean:

b. I like bread. (**general concept**)

Or:

c. I like **THE** bread. (e.g., **the one** on the table)

When talking about things that one likes, one usually uses the definite article, for example:

a. J'aime le fromage.
I like cheese.

b. J'aime la salade.
I like salad.

Do not forget about **elisions** with nouns that start with a vowel:

a. L'étudiant
The student

b. L'ampoule
The light bulb

EXERCISES
EXERCICES

1. Listen to the text and fill in the gaps. *Écoutez le texte et remplissez les trous.*

Je regarde (_____) film à (_____) télévision. Il y a (_____) scientifique qui rencontre (_____) investisseur. Ils décident de signer (_____) contrat ensemble pour cloner (_____) dinosaures et d'autres animaux qui ont disparu. Ensuite, (_____) scientifique et ses deux enfants sont sur (_____) île magnifique. (_____) oiseaux de l'île sont magnifiques et colorés. (_____) film est très intéressant. Mon frère n'a que huit ans et (_____) dinosaures lui font peur donc il arrête de regarder quand (_____) premiers dinosaures apparaissent.

Pendant (_____) film, (_____) amis de mes parents arrivent et nous regardons (_____) télévision ensemble. (_____)'amie de ma mère n'aime pas (_____) café donc elle boit du thé. Mon père boit (_____) verre de lait.

Après (_____) film, nous allons marcher dans (_____) forêt. Nous ne marchons qu'une heure car c'est bientôt (_____) nuit. (_____) voiture et (_____) tracteur passent devant nous. Ce sont des amis du village. (_____) nuit tombe donc nous devons rentrer à (_____) maison. Bonne nuit.

Translation

I am watching a movie on television. There is a scientist who meets an investor. They decide to sign a contract together to clone dinosaurs and other animals that have disappeared. Then, the scientist and his two children are on a beautiful island. The birds of the island are magnificent and colorful. The movie is very interesting. My brother is only eight years old and dinosaurs scare him, so he stops watching when the first dinosaurs appeared.

During the movie, some of my parents' friends arrive and we watch television together. My mother's friend does not like coffee so she drinks tea. My father drinks a glass of milk.

After the movie, we go and have a walk in the forest. We only walk for an hour because it is almost nighttime. A car and a tractor pass by. They are friends from the village. It is now nighttime, so we have to go inside the house. Good night.

CONTRACTED ARTICLES
ARTICLES CONTRACTÉS

When **de** and **à** are followed by **le** or **les**, they become **contracted**. The rules are the following:

   a. de + **le** becomes **du**

   b. à + **le** becomes **au**

   c. de + **les** becomes **des**

   d. à + **les** becomes **aux**

<u>**De** + **le** becoming **du** examples:</u>

   a. C'est la maison **du** professeur.
   It is the professor's house.

   b. C'est le nom **du** fromage.
   It is the name of the cheese.

   c. C'est l'adresse **du** bureau.
   It is the address of the office.

<u>**À** + **le** becoming **au** examples:</u>

   a. Nous sommes **au** restaurant.
   We are at the restaurant.

   b. Nous jouons **au** tennis.
   We play tennis.

   c. C'est une omelette **au** fromage.
   It is a cheese omelette.

De + les becoming **des** examples:

    a. C'est la chambre **des** parents.
       It is the parents' room.

    b. C'est le chat **des** voisins.
       It is the neighbors' cats.

    c. C'est la salle **des** professeurs.
       It is the professors' room.

Note that **des** is not necessarily a contraction of **de** + **les**. There is the **contracted des** (**de** + **les**) and the **indefinite des**.

For example:

    a. Des canards mangent du fromage.
       Some ducks eat cheese.

    b. Je parle des (de + les) canards.
       I speak about ducks.

In the previous examples, you can guess that **des** in the second sentence is a **contraction** of **de** + **les** if you ask yourself the question *De quoi parles-tu ?*

Then, you start answering the question by saying *Je parle de les canards*, and then you realize that **de** + **les** is **wrong** and that it should be **des**. This is the mnemonics taught in most schools throughout the French-speaking world to pupils when they are about 5 to 7 years old.

À + les becoming **aux** examples:

    a. L'enseignant parle **aux** enfants.
       The teacher talks to the children.

    b. J'aime la tarte **aux** pommes.
       I like apple pie.

    c. Il téléphone **aux** amis de son frère.
       He's calling his brother's friends.

When **à** and **de** are followed by **l'**, they are **not contracted**:

a. Il n'y avait personne **à l'**arrivée.
There was nobody on the finish line.

b. Je mange une tarte **à l'**abricot.
I eat an apricot pie.

c. Je suis **à l'**aéroport de Dublin.
I am at Dublin Airport.

d. Elle rentre de l'école.
She is coming back from school.

e. Il parle de l'amour.
He is taking about love.

« C'EST » ET « CE SONT »

In this section, you are going to learn about a challenging yet necessary concept to describe or identify things. To introduce something or someone to someone else, we use:

a. Singular: **c'est**

b. Plural: **ce sont**

For example:

a. **C'est** mon ami.
This is my friend.

b. **Ce sont** mes amis.
These are my friends.

Second example:

a. **C'est** une pomme.
This is an apple.

b. **Ce sont** des pommes.
These are apples.

Considering that this concept is unique in French, translating those expressions can be tricky. In the previous examples, **c'est** could also be translated as **that is** or **it is** and **ce sont** could also be translated as **those are** or **they are**. *It all depends on the context.*

When asking what something is, you only use the **singular** version of the expression. Therefore, even when there are several elements and you want to ask what they are, the singular form should be used.

For example:

a. Qu'est-ce que **c'est** ?
What are these?

b. Ce sont des poires.

These are pears.

To say who you are when talking on the **phone**, you should also use the **singular** form even if you are several people on one side of the line, for example:

a. Bonjour Bobby.

Hello Bobby.

Note: 'Allo' is a common greeting in French used when answering the phone.

b. Allo, qui **est-ce** ?

Hello, who's talking?

c. C'est Grégoire.

It's Grégoire.

C'est is also used to describe **general things** all the time in French.

a. C'est bon.

It's delicious.

b. C'est beau.

It is beautiful.

Those are general fixed expressions used even when talking about feminine and/or plural things.

For example:

a. Les étoiles, **c'est beau**.

Stars are beautiful.

b. Les voitures de sport, **c'est très cher**.

Sports cars are very expensive.

As you can see in these two examples, neither **beau** nor **cher** are in their plural form, which should be **beaux** or **chers**. Now, an example with feminine nominal groups and these fixed expressions:

a. La salade, **c'est bon**.

Salad is delicious.

---

b. La glace, **c'est froid**.
Ice is cold.

In these examples, neither **bon** or **froid** are in their feminine form, which would be **bonne** ou **froide**.

C'est and **ce sont** are also used to answer the following question:

a. Qui **est-ce** ? **C'est** Mario.
Who is that? That is Mario.

b. Qui **est-ce** ? **C'est** mon ami.
Who is that? That is my friend.

c. Qui **est-ce** ? **Ce sont** mes parents.
Who is that? Those are my parents.

With **il/elle est**, you usually **cannot** use an article in front of the noun. This is usually the case when talking about professional activities.

For example:

a. Correct: Il est médecin.
He is a doctor.

b. Not correct: Il est **un** médecin — wrong

If there is an adjective, then you probably need to use the **c'est** instead of **il/elle est**.

For example:

a. C'est un bon médecin.
He/she is a good doctor.

The same applies to a lot of other nouns.

For example:

a. Correct: **C'est** mon ami.
He/she is my friend.

b. Wrong: **Il/elle est** mon ami(e).

 **EXERCISES**
EXERCICES

1. **Fill in the gaps with "c'est" or "ce sont"**. *Remplissez les trous avec c'est ou ce sont.*

    a. _____ des arbres.
      These are trees.

    b. _____ des animaux.
      These are animals.

    c. Les documentaires, _____ intéressant.
      Documentaries are interesting.

    d. _____ une maison.
      This is a house.

    e. _____ une tortue.
      This is a turtle.

    f. _____ du fromage.
      This is cheese.

    g. L'écologie, _____ un sujet passionnant.
      Ecology is a fascinating subject.

    h. _____ des téléphones portables.
      These are mobile phones.

    i. _____ des chats.
      These are cats.

    j. Allo, bonjour Pierre, _____ tes amis au téléphone.
      Hello Pierre, your friends talking on the phone.

    k. _____ un arbre.
      This is a tree.

    l. Les chats, _____ mignon.
      Cats are cute.

    m. _____ des tasses.
      These are cups.

n. _____ un cheval.
This is a horse.

o. _____ une vache.
This is a cow.

2. **Answer the question "Qui est-ce ?" with full sentences.** _Répondez à la question "Qui est-ce ?" avec des phrases complètes._

Example:

my brother

C'est mon frère. / That is my brother.

Your turn:

the old man

_____

my cousin Lili

_____

my neighbor

_____

my parents

_____

my math teacher

_____

POSSESSIVES
LES POSSESSIFS

In French, possessive adjectives **agree** with the nouns they modify.

POSSESSIVE ADJECTIVES
ADJECTIFS POSSESSIFS

MASCULINE POSSESSIVES	
mon	my
ton	your
son	his/her/its
notre	our
votre	your
leur	their

For example:

a. **Mon** ami est allemand.
My friend is German.

b. **Ton** mari est norvégien.
Your husband is Norwegian.

c. **Son** professeur a un doctorat.
His/her professor has a PhD.

d. **Notre** canard est très vieux.
Our duck is very old.

e. **Votre** maison est tellement belle.
Your house is so beautiful.

f. **Leur** arbre est au milieu du jardin.
Their tree is in the middle of the garden.

As you can see in all these examples, the nouns that follow the possessive adjectives are masculine and singular nouns.

FEMININE POSSESSIVES	
ma	my
ta	your
sa	his/her/its
notre	our
votre	your
leur	their

For example:

a. Ma grand-mère a 75 ans.
My grandmother is 75 years old.

b. Ta voiture est rouge et bleue.
Your car is red and blue.

c. Sa chaise est cassée depuis hier.
His/her chair has been broken since yesterday.

d. Notre télévision est toute neuve.
Our television is brand new.

e. Votre cheminée est en briques rouges.
Your fireplace is made of red bricks.

f. Leur fleur est étrange.
Their flower is strange.

In these examples, the nouns that follow the possessive adjectives are feminine and singular.

PLURAL POSSESSIVES	
mes	my
tes	your
ses	his/her/its
nos	our
vos	your
leurs	their

For example:

a. **Mes** parents sont polyglottes.
My parents are polyglots.

b. **Tes** chaussettes sont propres.
Your socks are clean.

c. **Ses** sacs sont recyclables.
His/her bags are reusable.

d. **Nos** chaussures sont blanches.
Our shoes are white.

e. **Vos** chemises sont vertes.
Your shirts are green.

f. **Leurs** jouets sont chers.
Their toys are expensive.

In the previous examples, all the nouns that follow the possessive adjectives are plural nouns and whether they are masculine or feminine does not matter.

Please note that "**ma**", "**ta**", and "**sa**" become "**mon**", "**ton**", and "**son**", respectively, when they are followed **by a vowel or a silent h**.

For example:

a. **Mon a**rdoise vient d'Ardèche.
My slate comes from Ardèche.

b. **Ton a**mie raconte des histoires intéressantes.
Your female friend tells interesting stories.

c. Il a perdu deux points à cause de **son e**rreur.
He lost two points because of his mistake.

d. Mon héritière, c'est ma fille.
My daughter is my heir.

As you can see, in those cases, the possessed noun is a **feminine** noun, but the possessive used is **mon**.

POSSESSIVE PRONOUNS
PRONOMS POSSESSIFS

Like possessive adjectives, possessive pronouns **change according to the things they replace**.

MASCULINE SINGULAR	
le mien	mine
le tien	yours
le sien	his/hers
le nôtre	ours
le vôtre	yours
le leur	theirs

A use case for all these would be answering the question **À qui est ce manteau ?** (*Whose coat is this?*), **manteau** being a masculine singular noun.

FEMININE SINGULAR	
la mienne	mine
la tienne	yours
la sienne	his/hers
la nôtre	ours
la vôtre	yours
la leur	theirs

The elements of the first column could be used to answer the question **À qui est cette voiture?** (*Whose car is this?*), **voiture** being a feminine singular noun.

MASCULINE PLURAL	
les miens	mine
les tiens	yours
les siens	his/hers
les nôtres	ours
les vôtres	yours
les leurs	theirs

Those could be used to answer the question **À qui sont ces chats ?** (*Whose cats are these?*) **chats** being a masculine plural noun.

FEMININE PLURAL	
les miennes	mine
les tiennes	yours
les siennes	his/hers
les nôtres	ours
les vôtres	yours
les leurs	theirs

You may have already noticed that in the possessive **pronouns**, **nôtre** and **vôtre** are written with an **ô** whereas as the possessive **adjectives** they are written as **notre** and **votre**:

a. C'est votre voiture.
   That is your car.

b. Oui, c'est **la vôtre**.
   Yes, it is yours.

c. C'est notre maison.
   That is our house.

d. Oui, c'est **la nôtre**.
   Yes, that is ours.

EXERCISES
EXERCICES

1. Fill in the gaps with the correct possessive adjectives, like in the examples. *Remplissez les trous avec l'adjectif possessif correct comme dans les exemples.*

Examples:

Je (le vélo) : C'est le mien.
It is his bicycle.

Pierre (la fleur) : C'est la sienne.
It is your flower.

Your turn:

a. Je : C'est _____ sac.
It is my bag.

b. Alexandre : Ce sont _____ ordinateurs.
These are their computers.

c. Vous : Ce sont _____ jouets et _____ paniers.
These are their toys and their baskets.

d. David : C'est _____ téléscope.
It is her telescope.

e. Elles : C'est _____ jardin.
It is your garden.

f. Mr. Michel : C'est _____ crayon.
It is your pencil.

g. Ils : C'est _____ chien.
It is his dog.

h. Mme André : C'est _____ ami.
It is their friend.

2. **Answer the question "Whose is it?" or "Whose are these?" with the correct possessive pronouns, like in the example.** *Pay careful attention to whether the nouns are in their singular or plural forms. Répondez à la question "À qui est-ce ?" avec le pronom possessif correct comme dans l'exemple. Attention aux noms qui peuvent être au singulier ou au pluriel.*

Examples:

Je (vélo) : C'est le mien.
It is mine. (bicycle)

Pierre (fleur) : C'est la sienne.
It is his. (flower)

Your turn:

    a. Je (téléphone) : _____.
      It is mine. (phone)

    b. Alexandre (microscopes) : _____.
      They are his. (microscopes)

    c. Vous (pomme) : _____.
      It is yours. (apple)

    d. David (thé) : _____.
      It is his. (tea)

    e. Elles (tables) : _____.
      These are theirs. (tables)

    f. Mr. Michel (lunettes) : _____.
      These are his. (glasses)

    g. Ils (lampe) : _____.
      It is theirs. (lamp)

    h. Mme André (clavier) : _____.
      It is hers. (keyboard)

NOUNS RELATED TO RELATIVES AND SENSE OF BELONGING
LES NOMS DE PARENTÉS ET DE GROUPE

In this section, you are going to learn how to talk about **family members**. Here is some preliminary vocabulary:

a. Le père
The father

b. La mère
The mother

c. Les parents
The parents

d. La grand-mère
The grandmother

e. Le grand-père
The grandfather

f. Les grands-parents
The grandparents

g. La petite-fille
The granddaughter

h. Le petit-fils
The grandson

i. Les petits-enfants
The grandchildren

j. La tante
The aunt

k. L'oncle
The uncle

l. La nièce
The niece

m. Le neveu
The nephew

n. Les neveux
The nieces and nephews

o. La grand-tante
The great-aunt

p. Le grand-oncle
The great-uncle

q. La petite-nièce
The great-niece

r. Le petit neveu
The great-nephew

As you may have noticed, **petit** (*small*) is used to refer to **descendants** (younger ones) whereas **grand** (*big*) is used to refer to the **older ones**.

Note: In French, the word **parents** can mean two things depending on the context, it can mean parents as in mother and father, but it can also mean relatives.

For example:

    a. Les parents de Pierre sont âgés.
       Pierre's parents are old.

    b. Des parents de Michel seront présents au mariage.
       Some of Michel's relatives will attend the wedding.

Now, you are going to learn some words to describe your family by marriage. The French words can be confusing to English speakers because some of them can refer to **two different concepts**:

    a. La **belle-mère** : either the **mother-in-law** or the **stepmother**.

    b. Le **beau-père** : either the **father-in-law** or the **stepfather**.

    c. La **belle-fille** : either the **daughter-in-law** or the **stepdaughter**.

    d. Le **beau-fils** : either the **son-in-law** or the **stepson**.

The other words are easier:

    a. La belle-sœur
       The sister-in-law

    b. Le beau-frère
       The brother-in-law

1. Answer the questions like in the example. *Répondez aux questions comme dans l'exemple.*

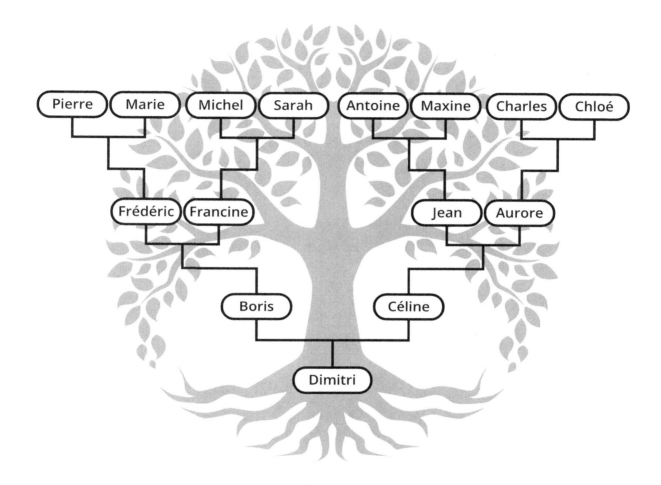

First example:

Qui est Pierre pour Marie ? C'est **son mari**. / *Who is Pierre for Marie? He is her husband.*

Second example:

Qui est Francine pour Pierre et Marie ? C'est **leur belle-fille**. / *Who is Francine for Pierre and Marie? She is their daughter-in-law.*

Your turn:

a. Qui est Boris pour Pierre, Marie, Michel et Sarah ? C'est _____.
Who is Boris for Pierre, Marie, Michel, and Sarah? He is their grandson.

b. Qui est Maxine pour Céline ? C'est _____.
Who is Maxine for Céline? She is her grandmother.

c. Qui est Chloé pour Aurore ? C'est _____.
Who is Chloé for Aurore? She is her mother.

d. Qui est Céline pour Boris ? C'est _____.
Who is Céline for Boris? She is his wife.

e. Qui est Dimitri pour Boris et Céline ? C'est _____.
Who is Dimitri for Boris and Céline? He is their son.

f. Qui est Aurore pour Maxine et Antoine ? C'est _____.
Who is Aurore for Maxine and Antoine? She is their daughter-in-law.

g. Qui est Frédéric pour Michel et Sarah ? C'est _____.
Who is Frédéric for Michel and Sarah? He is their son-in-law.

2. **Introduce your family**. *Présentez votre famille.*

For example:

Jean est mon mari. Pierre est mon frère. Marie est ma sœur. Marc est mon beau-frère, etc. /
Jean is my husband. Pierre is my brother. Marie is my sister. Marc is my brother-in-law, etc.

Your turn:

_____

_____

_____

_____

DEMONSTRATIVES
LES DÉMONSTRATIFS

DEMONSTRATIVE ADJECTIVE
ADJECTIF DÉMONSTRATIF

In French, demonstrative adjectives function similarly to the English words "this," "that," "these," and "those. Unlike in English, **demonstrative adjectives** have to agree in gender and number with the noun to which they refer.

For example:

    a. **Ce stylo** can either mean **this pen** or **that pen**.

    b. **Cette voiture** can either mean **this car** or **that car**.

    c. **Ces oiseaux** can either mean **these birds** or **those birds**.

Also, unlike in English, the difference between **this** and **that** is not as straightforward and often depends on the context. **-ci** and **-là** are used.

For example:

    a. **Cette année-ci**, nous sommes allés au Canada.
       We went to Canada this year.

    b. **Cette année-là**, nous étions encore jeunes.
       We were still young that year.

DEMONSTRATIVE PRONOUN
PRONOM DÉMONSTRATIF

Demonstrative pronouns are usually **used to avoid repeating the same things**.

<u>Examples with **-ci** to express closeness in time or in space:</u>

a. C'est mon chat. **Celui-ci** est à mon ami.
This is my cat. This one is my friend's.

b. C'est ma maison. **Celle-ci** est à mon frère.
This is my house. This one is my brother's.

c. Ce sont mes chiens. **Ceux-ci** sont à mes parents.
These are my dogs. These are my parents'.

d. Ce sont mes plantes. **Celles-ci** sont à mes frères.
These are my plants. These are my brothers'.

<u>Same examples with **-là** to express distance in time or physical distance:</u>

a. C'est mon chat. **Celui-là** est à mon ami.
This is my cat. That one is my friend's.

b. C'est ma maison. **Celle-là** est à mon frère.
This is my house. That one is my brother's.

c. Ce sont mes chiens. **Ceux-là** sont à mes parents.
These are my dogs. Those are my parents'.

d. Ce sont mes plantes. **Celles-là** sont à mes frères.
These are my plants. Those are my brothers'.

Celui and **celle** can also be used individually to express **possession**.

For example:

    a. À qui est ce chien ? C'est **celui** de mon frère.
       Whose dog is this? It is my brother's.

    b. À qui est cette maison ? C'est **celle** de mon père.
       Whose house is this? It is my father's.

    c. À qui sont ces ordinateurs ? Ce sont **ceux** de ma mère.
       Whose computers are these? They are my mother's.

    d. À qui sont ces voitures ? Ce sont **celles** de ma sœur.
       Whose cars are these? They are my sister's.

In the previous example, **these** can be replaced by **those,** depending on the context. Some context can be added to the questions by adding **-ci** or **-là** to the nouns. For example, the first question could have been asked this way:

    a. À qui est ce **chien-ci** ?
       Whose dog is this?

Or:

    a. À qui est ce **chien-là** ?
       Whose dog is that?

 **EXERCISES**
EXERCICES

1. Fill in the gaps with the proper demonstrative, like in the example. *Remplissez les trous avec le démonstratif adéquat comme dans l'exemple.*

Example:

    Cette tasse est petite.
    This cup is small.

Your turn:

    a. _____ livre est intéressant.
    This book is interesting.

    b. _____ fleur est belle.
    This flower is pretty.

    c. _____ villages sont petits.
    These villages are small.

    d. _____ bouteilles sont lourdes.
    These bottles are heavy.

    e. _____ assiettes sont vertes.
    These plates are green.

    f. _____ casquette est blanche.
    This cap is white.

    g. _____ porte est blindée.
    This door is bulletproof.

    h. _____ arbre est vieux.
    This tree is old.

    i. _____ chat aime jouer.
    This cat likes playing.

2. Listen and fill in the gaps with the correct possessive, like in the example.
Écoutez et remplissez les trous avec le possessif adéquat comme dans l'exemple.
(Find audio on page 12.)

Example:

À qui est cette table ? C'est **celle** de mon ami.
Whose table is this? It is my friend's.

Your turn:

a. À qui est ce canard ? C'est _____ de mon voisin.
Whose duck is this? It is my neighbor's.

b. À qui est cet éléphant ? C'est _____ du maire.
Whose elephant is that? It is the mayor's.

c. À qui est cette boîte ? C'est _____ de ma grand-mère.
Whose box is this? It is my grandmother's.

d. À qui est ce téléphone portable ? C'est _____ de mon mari.
Whose mobile phone is this? It is my husband's.

e. À qui sont ces billets ? Ce sont _____ de mon patron.
Whose banknotes are these? They are my boss'.

f. À qui est cette couverture ? C'est _____ de mes parents.
Whose blanket is this? It is my parents'.

« IL Y A » AND « C'EST »

Unlike in English, the verb **avoir** (*to have*) is used to express **that something exists**. We call such a construct an <u>impersonal construct.</u>

Il y a is used to describe that **something exists**.

For example:

    a. Il y a un chat sur la table.
      There is a cat on the table.

    b. Il y a une assiette dans le lave-vaisselle.
      There is a plate in the dishwasher.

In the two previous examples, you can see that the location is indicated but <u>you do not need to specify where the described things are:</u>

    a. Il y a des gens.
      There are people.

You can also specify a <u>certain date or timing:</u>

    a. Il y a un débat politique à la télévision à 8 h du soir.
      There is a political debate on television at 8 PM.

As you can see in the previous example, **il y a** can be followed by **masculine** or **feminine** as well as **singular** or **plural** forms:

    a. Il y a **un**

    b. Il y a **une**

    c. Il y a **des**

In the previous sections, you learned about **c'es**t and **ce sont**. These expressions can be used to describe something you have just introduced with **il y a**.

For example:

    a. Il y a un arbre dans le champ. **C'est** un cyprès.
       There is a tree in the field. It is a cypress.

    b. Il y a des animaux dans le jardin. **Ce sont** des poules.
       There are animals in the garden. They are hens.

As mentioned above, we call this construct an impersonal construct because the subject **il** <u>does not refer to anyone or anything.</u>

EXERCISES
EXERCICES

1. **Fill in the gaps with either "il y a" or "c'est", or "ce sont". Put an X when no article is required.** *Remplissez les trous avec "il y a", "c'est" ou "ce sont". Mettez un X si aucun article n'est requis.*

   a. _____ des fleurs dans le champ. _____ des roses. Elles sont très belles.
   There are flowers in the field. They are roses. They are very beautiful.

   b. _____ une table dans le salon. _____ une table ancienne. Elle est en bois.
   There is a table in the living room. It is an old table. It is made of wood

   c. _____ un film à la télévision. _____ Casablanca. Mes parents l'aiment beaucoup.
   There is a movie on television. It is Casablanca. My parents like it a lot.

   d. _____ un grand trou dans le jardin. _____ l'endroit où la piscine sera.
   There is a big hole in the garden. It is where the swimming-pool will be.

EXPRESSING LOCATIONS
SITUER DANS L'ESPACE

Talking about places such as *cities* (**les villes**), *countries* (**les pays**), and *continents* (**les continents**) can be challenging in many languages. It is also the case in French. Some countries have *articles where most others do not:*

a. France

b. The United States of America

c. The Gambia

d. The Netherlands

e. China

In French, names of cities are *usually not preceded by an article:*

a. Paris / *Paris*

c. Sofia / *Sofia*

b. Montréal / *Montreal*

d. Zürich / *Zurich*

However:

a. Le Touquet / *Le Touquet*

b. La Rochelle / *La Rochelle*

c. Le Caire / *Cairo*

We recommend that you learn the proper article each time you learn the name of a new city. For that purpose, when you know the name of a place in English, you can first look it up in a dictionary that includes proper nouns. and if you cannot find it there, you can look it up on Wikipedia and then switch the language to French to see the equivalent article in French. You should be able to see whether there is an article there. Of course, feel free to ask your French-speaking friends as well!

Countries and continents are *usually preceded by an article.*

The continents:

a. **L'**Afrique / *Africa*

b. **L'**Amérique du Sud / *South America*

c. **L'**Amérique du Nord / *North America*

d. **L'**Europe / *Europe*

e. **L'**Asie / *Asia*

f. **L'**Océanie / *Oceania*

g. **L'**Antarctique / *Antarctica*

Note that there is an **elision** when it comes to all those continents. **La + *Europe*** becomes **L'Europe,** but *Europe* is feminine. The European Union translates as *L'Union Européen**ne*** in French, for example. The same applies to *Asie*. For example, *Anatolia* translates as *L'Asie Mineur**e*** (*Mineure* with an **-e**, feminine form). To sum up, all continents are feminine in French.

When it comes to countries, some are preceded by an article while some others are not.

Some examples of countries that are preceded by an article:

a. **La** France / *France*

b. **Le** Canada / *Canada*

c. **Les** États-Unis d'Amérique / *The United States of America*

d. **La** Jamaïque / *Jamaica*

e. **L'**Ouganda (masculine) / *Uganda*

f. **L'**Inde (feminine) / *India*

Examples of countries that do not have an article:

a. **Maurice** (feminine) / *Mauritius*

b. **Malte** (feminine) / *Malta*

c. **Bahreïn** (masculine) / *Bahrain*

d. **Saint-Marin** (masculine) / *San Marino*

In French, there are often exceptions. Some countries *can be preceded by an article or not*:

For example, you can say either "Brunéi Darussalam" <u>or</u> "**Le** Brunéi Darussalam" both regarded as masculine. / *Brunei Darussalam*

The *gender can even change* depending on whether you use an article or not:

"**Le** Sri Lanka" is masculine, whereas "Sri Lanka" without an article is considered feminine. / *Sri Lanka*

When you have the choice whether to use an article or not like in the two previous examples, feel free to choose whichever form you like as they refer to the same thing.

Beware, many countries which end with an **-e** seem to be feminine but it is not always the case:

    a. La Suiss**e** (feminine)
       Switzerland

But:

    b. Le Cambodg**e** (masculine)
       Cambodia

To indicate where you are, you usually use **à** for cities and countries *that do not have an article.* Here are a few examples with *cities that do not have an article:*

    a. Je suis **à** Barcelone.
       I am in Barcelona.

    b. Mes parents sont **à** Tokyo.
       My parents are in Tokyo.

    c. Mon frère est **à** Brisbane.
       My brother is in Brisbane.

Here are a few examples with countries *which do not have an article:*

    a. Hélène est **à** Saint-Marin.
       Hélène is in San Marino.

    b. Jean-François est **à** Malte.
       Jean-François is in Malta.

    c. Tristan est **à** Maurice.
       Tristan is in Mauritius.

If you chose to talk about Brunei Darussalam without an article, you would also say:

a. Martin est **à** Brunéi Darussalam.
Martin is in Brunei Darussalam.

When talking about a *masculine country that has an article*, you need to use **au + the country name**:

a. Nous sommes **au** Japon.
We are in Japan.

b. Vous êtes **au** Canada.
You are in Canada.

When talking about a country whose *article is in the plural form*, you use **aux + the country name**:

a. Il est **aux** États-Unis.
He is in the United States.

b. Elles sont **aux** Pays-Bas.
They (feminine, plural) are in the Netherlands.

c. Ken est **aux** Philippines.
Ken is in the Philippines.

When talking about countries whose *article is in the feminine form*, you use **en + the country name**:

a. Paul est **en** France.
Paul is in France.

b. Marc est **en** Pologne.
Marc is in Poland.

c. Jacques est **en** Bolivie.
Jacques is in Bolivia.

Finally, when talking about *continents*, you simply use **en + the name of the continent**:

a. Je suis **en** Europe.
I am in Europe.

b. Tu es **en** Amérique du Nord.
You (singular) are in North America.

c. Nous sommes **en** Océanie.
We are in Oceania.

d. Vous êtes **en** Afrique.
You (plural) are in Africa.

e. Ils sont **en** Antarctique.
They are in Antarctica.

f. Mon frère est **en** Asie.
My brother is in Asia.

Note: **en** is used in front of *countries which start with a vowel, even if* they are masculine and singular:

a. Correct: **en** Iran
In Iran

b. Not correct: à l'Iran or au Iran

When a city *has an article and is feminine*, you use **à**:

a. Je suis **à** La Rochelle.
I am in La Rochelle.

When a city *has an article and is masculine*, you use **au**:

a. Je suis **au** Havre.
I am in Le Havre.

EXERCISES
EXERCICES

1. **Fill in the gaps with the correct article. Put an X when no article is required.** *Remplissez les trous avec le bon article. Mettez un X si aucun article n'est requis.*

    a. _____ Japon est connu pour sa cuisine, son cinéma et ses îles.
    Japan is known for its cuisine, its cinema, and its islands.

    b. _____ Malte est une île qui se trouve en Europe. Son climat est sec et chaud.
    Malta is an island that is situated in Europe. Its climate is dry and warm.

    c. _____ Chine est un des plus grands pays du monde. C'est un pays avec plus de 8000 ans d'histoire.
    China is one of the biggest countries in the world. It is a country with over 8,000 years of history.

    d. _____ Maurice n'est pas loin de La Réunion, une île française.
    Mauritius is not far from Réunion, a French island.

    e. _____ Cuba est un pays qui produit beaucoup de cigares.
    Cuba is a country that produces many cigars.

    f. _____ Bulgarie est le pays des roses.
    Bulgaria is the country of roses.

    g. _____ Philippines ont des îles paradisiaques.
    The Philippines has paradisiacal islands.

    h. _____ Pays-Bas sont un pays où il n'y a pas beaucoup de montagnes.
    The Netherlands is a country where there are not many mountains.

2. **Answer the questions with the country and continent.** *Répondez aux questions avec le pays et le continent.*

    a. Où se trouve la Statue de la Liberté ?
    Where is the Statue of Liberty?

    La Statue de la Liberté se trouve _____ États-Unis, _____ Amérique du Nord.
    The Statue of Liberty is in the United States, in North America.

b. Où se trouve la Tour Eiffel ?
Where is the Eiffel Tower?

La Tour Eiffel se trouve _____ France, _____ Europe.
The Eiffel Tower is in France, in Europe.

c. Où se trouve la Grande Muraille ?
Where is the Great Wall?

La Grande Muraille se trouve _____ Chine, _____ Asie.
The Great Wall is in China, in Asia.

d. Où se trouve Berne ?
Where is Bern?

Berne est _____ Suisse, _____ Europe.
Bern is in Switzerland, in Europe.

e. Où se trouve la Tour de Pise ?
Where is the Tower of Pisa?

La Tour de Pise se trouve _____ Italie, _____ Europe.
The Tower of Pisa is in Italy, in Europe.

f. Où se trouvent les chutes du Niagara ?
Where are the Niagara Falls?

Les chutes du Niagara sont _____ États-Unis et _____ Canada, _____ Amérique du Nord.
The Niagara Falls are in the United States and Canada, in North America.

NUMBERS
LES NOMBRES

In this chapter, you are going to learn about numbers in general.

CARDINAL NUMBERS
LES NOMBRES CARDINAUX

First, here is how to count **from one to nineteen**:

un	one	**dix**	ten
deux	two	**onze**	eleven
trois	three	**douze**	twelve
quatre	four	**treize**	thirteen
cinq	five	**quatorze**	fourteen
six	six	**quinze**	fifteen
sept	seven	**seize**	sixteen
huit	eight	**dix-sept**	seventeen
neuf	nine	**dix-huit**	eighteen
		dix-neuf	nineteen

Now, things get a little bit more complicated from twenty. So, first, here are the multiples of ten:

vingt	twenty	**soixante**	sixty
trente	thirty	**soixante-dix**	seventy
quarante	forty	**quatre-vingts**	eighty
cinquante	fifty	**quatre-vingt-dix**	ninety
cent	hundred		

As you can see, the multiples of ten are quite straightforward until **seventy**. The rules are the following:

a. For **70**, you have to take **sixty (60)** and add **ten (10)** which makes: **soixante + dix = soixante-dix**

b. For **80**, you have to multiply **four (4)** by **twenty (20)** which makes: **quatre** x **vingt = quatre-vingts**

c. For **90**, you have to multiply four by twenty and add **10**: **quatre** x **vingt + dix = quatre-vingt-dix**

Pay careful attention to the spelling of these numbers; there is an **-s** at the end of **quatre-vingts** but there is no **-s** at the end of **vingt** in **quatre-vingt-dix.**

You are now going to learn how to add one to all those multiples of ten. Once again, it is not as straightforward as in English, so you also need to learn them by heart. But do not worry, once you know how it works until one hundred, you will be able to count to infinity, or almost!

Vingt et un	Twenty-one	Soixante et un	Sixty-one
Trente et un	Thirty-one	Soixante et onze	Seventy-one
Quarante et un	Forty-one	Quatre-vingt-un	Eighty-one
Cinquante et un	Fifty-one	Quatre-vingt-onze	Ninety-one

As you can see in this table, it is straightforward from **vingt** (*twenty*) to **soixante** (*sixty*) but becomes, once again, complicated from **soixante-dix** (*seventy*). Actually, you may have noticed that there is a pattern here that immediately makes everything easier? Have you seen it yet?

No?

Well done if you recognized the pattern! If you have not, no problem, French grammar can be challenging at times. Do you remember in the previous table how you learned about the *multiples* *of ten*? It was also starting to become more complicated from **soixante-dix** (*seventy*); but if you remember that seventy is **soixante-dix**, <u>then you will also notice that:</u>

    a. Seventy-one is **soixante** (*sixty*) et **onze** (*eleven*) because you take **soixante-dix** and adds *one* to **dix** (*ten*): **soixante + dix + one = soixante + onze = soixante et onze**

And then you will also notice that **quatre-vingt-dix** (*ninety*) also works in the same way:

    a. Ninety-one is **quatre-vingts** (*eighty*) and **onze** (*eleven*) because you take **quatre-vingts** (*eighty*) and add **one** to **dix** (*ten*): quatre-vingt-dix + one = **quatre-vingt-onze** (*ninety-one*)

Note that **quatre-vingt** (*eighty*) works like the other numbers from **quatre-vingt-un** (*eighty-one*) to **quatre-vingt-neuf** (*eighty-nine*). You just need to replace the last number by **deux** (*two*), **trois** (*three*), etc., respectively.

The same applies to **soixante-dix** (*seventy*) and **quatre-vingt-dix** (*ninety*), you just need to replace the dix by onze, douze, treize, etc., respectively.

For example:

    a. *Seventy-six* becomes **soixante-seize**

    b. *Ninety-five* becomes **quatre-vingt-quinze**

Then, *one hundred* is **cent**. The multiples of **cent** (*one hundred*) are easy to build, you just add the desired number in front of **cent** and add an **-s** to cent.

For example:

Cent	One hundred
Deux cents	Two hundred
Trois cents	Three hundred
Neuf cents	Nine hundred

To construct the numbers in between, it is quite straightforward, you just add all the numbers you just learned after cent (*one hundred*) and its respective multiples.

For example:

Cent un	One hundred
Deux cent trente	Two hundred thirty
Quatre cent soixante et un	Four hundred sixty-one
Six cent soixante-dix	Six hundred seventy
Huit cent quatre-vingts	Eight hundred eighty
Neuf cent quatre-vingt-dix-neuf	Nine hundred ninety-nine

As you can see, there are no particular challenges here except that **cent** (*one hundred*) loses its **-s** when it's followed by something else. Understanding why is out of scope in this book though.

Then, from **mille** (*a thousand*) to **un milliard** (*one billion*), there are no particular challenges either.

Mille	One thousand	**Un million**	One million
Dix mille	Ten thousand	**Dix millions**	Ten million
Cent mille	One hundred thousand	**Un milliard**	One billion
		Dix milliards	Ten billion

The only thing you need to remember is that **million** (*million*) and **milliard** (*billion*) always agree in number.

    a. Un **million** (*one million*) but **deux millions** (*two million*)

    b. Un **milliard** (*one billion*) but **six milliards** (*six billion*)

Mille (*one thousand*), on the other hand, always remains invariable.

ORDINAL NUMBERS
LES NOMBRES

Ordinal numbers are used to talk about gradings, the results of a competition, the floors on a building...

For example:

    a. Le **deuxième** étage
       The second floor

    b. Il est arrivé **premier** de la course.
       He came first in the race.

In French, the general rule is that you take the cardinal number and you add **-ième** at the end to create an ordinal number:

    a. Trois   →   trois**ième**
       three   →   *third*

    b. Vingt   →   vingti**ème**
       Twenty   →   *twentieth*

There are a few exceptions, though; the cardinal number of **un** is irregular, **cinq** and **neuf** are a bit different as well:

    a. Un   →   premier
       one   →   *first*

b. Cinq   →   cin**qu**ième

    five   →   *fifth*

c. Neuf   →   neu**v**ième

    nine   →   *ninth*

For <u>numbers ending with an -e</u>, you need to remove the -e before you add **-ième**

a. Quatre   →   quatr**ième**

    Four   →   *fourth*

b. Onze   →   onzi**ème**

    eleven   →   *eleventh*

For <u>numbers ending with an -s</u>, you need to remove the -s before you add **-ième** also.

a. Quatre-vingts   →   quatre-vingtième

    eighty   →   *eightieth*

EXERCISES
EXERCICES

 **1. Listen to the sentences and fill in the blanks**. *Écoutez les phrases et complétez les trous.*

a. Vous pouvez m'appeler à ce numéro : _____

You can call me on this number:_____.

b. Pour aller au Trocadéro, il faut prendre la ligne _____ et _____

To go to the Trocadéro, you need to take line _____ and _____.

c. Ça vous fera _____.

That will be _____.

d. De Lyon, vous êtes à _____ kilomètres de Paris. Vous en avez pour

_____ de route.

From Lyon, you are _____ km away from Paris. It's a _____ drive.

2. Write the right ordinal number under each runner. *Écrivez le bon numéro ordinal sous chaque coureur.*

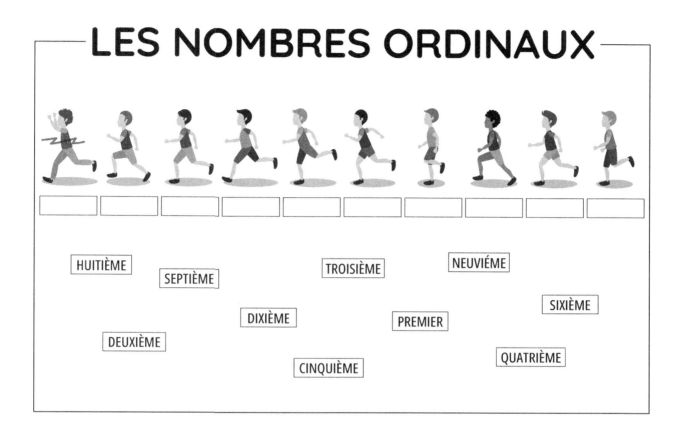

LES NOMBRES ORDINAUX

HUITIÈME

SEPTIÈME

TROISIÈME

NEUVIÉME

SIXIÈME

DIXIÈME

PREMIER

DEUXIÈME

QUATRIÈME

CINQUIÈME

TIME, DATE, AND WEATHER
LE TEMPS

When talking about le **jour de la semaine** (*day of the week*), we use **on est**, **nous sommes** or **c'est**.

For example:

a. Aujourd'hui, **on est lundi**.
   It is Monday.

b. Demain, **c'est mardi**.
   Tomorrow is Tuesday.

Les jours de la semaine
Days of the week:

a. **lundi**
   Monday

b. **mardi**
   Tuesday

c. **mercredi**
   Wednesday

d. **jeudi**
   Thursday

e. **vendredi**
   Friday

f. **samedi**
   Saturday

g. **dimanche**
   Sunday

Note that in French, the days of the week **are not capitalized** like in English unless they are, of course, in first position in a sentence.

a. Je n'aime pas le lundi.
   I don't like Mondays.

b. Le dimanche, c'est mon jour préféré de la semaine.
   Sunday is my favorite day of the week.

When talking about **la date** (*the date*), we usually use **on est**, **nous sommes**, or **c'est** as well.

For example:

a. **Nous sommes** le 15 janvier.
It is January 15.

b. **On est** le 21 juin.
It is June 21.

c. **C'est** le 23 mars.
It is March 23.

Like the days of the week, the names of the months **are not capitalized** unless they are in first position in a sentence. Moreover, like in American English, the number of the month in French is pronounced as such.

- So, in our first example, **15** is pronounced as **quinze** and not as **quinzième** (*fifteenth*).

- In the second example, **21** is pronounced as **vingt et un**.

The only **exception** to that rule is when talking about the **first day** of the month.

For example:

a. Nous sommes le **1er** février aujourd'hui.
Today is February 1st.

b. Aujourd'hui, c'est le **1er** avril.
Today is April 1st.

You probably noticed **-er** after **1**; **1er** is pronounced **premier** and means *first*. This is the **only** case where the ordinal number is used instead of the cardinal one.

When talking about **les jours de la semaine** (*the days of the week*) in a general way, one simply uses **le** followed by the day.

For example:

    a. Le dimanche, je fais la grasse matinée.
       I sleep in on Sundays.

    b. Le mercredi, je ne travaille pas.
       I do not work on Wednesdays.

When talking about **le moment de la journée** (*the time of the day*), one uses **le** followed by the time of the day.

For example:

    a. Le matin, je mange un croissant.
       I eat a croissant in the morning.

    b. Je fais de l'exercice **l'après-midi**.
       I exercise in the afternoon.

    c. Je lis un livre **le soir**.
       I read a book in the evening.

The same rule applies if you add a day of the week in the sentence.

For example:

    a. Je mange du pain **le** mercredi matin.
       I eat bread on Wednesday morning.

    b. Je travaille **le** vendredi soir.
       I work on Friday evening.

When talking about **les mois** (*months*) on their own, we use **en** to say that something happens in that month.

For example:

    a. En mars, il fait froid.   **b.** Il fait chaud **en** août.
       It is cold in March.   *It is hot in August.*

When saying which month it is, you either use **on est au mois de** or **nous sommes au mois de** or **on est en** or **nous sommes en**.

For example:

> **a. On est au mois de** janvier.
> *We are in January.*

> **b. Nous sommes au mois d'**avril.
> *We are in April.*

> **c. On est en** juillet.
> *It is July.*

> **d. Nous sommes en** septembre.
> *It is September.*

When talking about **les saisons** (*seasons*), you have to use **au** in front of a **consonant** and **en** in front of a **vowel** or a **silent h:**

> **a.** On est **en** hiver.
> *We are in winter.*

> **b.** Nous sommes **au** printemps.
> *We are in spring.*

> **c.** On est **en** été.
> *We are in summer.*

> **d.** Nous sommes **en** automne.
> *We are in fall.*

When talking about les années (years), we also use **en**.

For example:

> **a.** On est **en** 2015.
> *We are in 2015.*

When talking about **le temps** (*time*), we always use the singular form **il est** followed by the time.

For example:

    a. Il est dix heures.
      It is ten o'clock.

    b. Il est onze heures douze.
      It is eleven and twelve minutes.

    c. Il est quatorze heures trente-neuf.
      It is two and thirty-nine minutes.

As you can see in the previous example, in French, AM and PM **are not used**. Instead, we count from **1 to 23** and 00:00 or 12 AM is **minuit** and 12:00 or 12 PM is **midi**.

For example:

    a. Il est minuit cinq.
      It is 12:05 AM.

    b. Il est midi vingt-cinq.
      It is 12:25 PM.

    c. Il est vingt-trois heures.
      It is 11 PM.

    d. Il est une heure.
      It is 1 AM.

It is important to note that it is possible to use the numbers 1 to 11 by adding **du matin** (AM) or **du soir** (PM) after them, as you may hear in daily life, but this is more colloquial. Usually, in written French, what we said above prevails.

To say **quarter past, half past,** and a **quarter to**, we use, respectively, **et quart, et demie,** and **moins le quart**.

    a. Il est neuf heures **et quart**.
      It is a quarter past nine.

b. Il est dix heures **et demie**.

It is half past ten.

c. Il est midi **moins le quart**.

It is a quarter to twelve in the afternoon.

You may have noticed that **et demie** is written with an **-e** at the end, this is because it implies *a half hour* and **une heure** (*hour*) is feminine, hence the **-e.**

And the question to ask for the time, even if it is less and less used since most of us now have watches or mobile phones, is:

a. Quelle heure est-il ?

What time is it?

b. Le prochain bus part à quelle heure ?

What time does the next bus leave?

This form allows you to ask not only for the current time but also for the time when something is scheduled to happen.

In French, le temps can refer to the concepts of date and time, but it can also refer to the concept of **weather**. When you want to ask what the weather is like, you ask:

a. Quel temps fait-il ?

What is the weather like?

Learning to talk about the weather is always a great idea when speaking a foreign language. In most languages, talking about the weather is usual small talk.

To describe the weather, you use impersonal constructs. You have learned, in previous sections, what impersonal constructs are. You can either use **adjectives**, **nouns**, or **impersonal verbal constructs** to describe the weather. Here are some common constructs to describe the weather.

Using an adjective:

a. Il fait chaud.

It is hot.

b. Il fait froid.
It is cold.

c. Il fait beau.
The weather is nice.

d. Il ne fait pas beau.
The weather is not nice.

Using a noun:

a. Il y a du soleil.
It is sunny.

b. Il y a des nuages.
It is cloudy.

c. Il y a du vent.
It is windy.

As you can see, **soleil** (*sun*), **nuages** (*clouds*), and **vent** (*wind*) are nouns. As a reminder, **du** is the contraction of **de** + **le**. If you do not remember why or how to use that construct, refer to the previous sections.

Using a verb:

a. Il pleut cet après-midi.
It is raining this afternoon.

b. Il neige ce matin.
It is snowing this morning.

c. Il vente ce soir.
It is windy this evening.

Pleut in **il pleut** is the impersonal verb **pleuvoir** (*to rain*). **Neige** in **il neige** is the impersonal verb **neiger** (*to snow*). **Vente** in **il vente** is the impersonal verb **venter** (*to be windy*). These verbs are impersonal as they can only be used with an impersonal **il,** which does not refer to anyone.

Expressions are always fun when learning a foreign language and French speakers love to use expressions to talk about the weather. Here are two expressions that you do not necessarily have to learn but which are really funny.

First expression:

   a. Il fait un temps de chien.
   Literally: It is a dog's weather.

Can you guess what it means?

...

This expression started being used in the beginning of the twentieth century. Since dogs were mostly sleeping outside, even when the weather was really bad, people therefore started saying that to describe bad weather.

Second expression:

   b. Il fait un froid de canard.
   Literally: It is a duck's coldness.

What about this one? Did you guess what it means?

...

People supposedly started using this expression to describe really cold weather because duck hunting season takes place in the fall. In the regions were French-speaking hunters hunted ducks, it was usually really cold, especially at the end of the hunting season.

 **EXERCISES**
EXERCICES

1. Write the date in a full sentence. *Écrivez la date en une phrase complète.*

    a. 12/15/2022 _____

    b. 03/07/1902 _____

    c. 08/09/1972 _____

2. Write the time in a full sentence. *Écrivez l'heure en une phrase complète.*

3. Describe what the weather is like in France on the map. *Décrivez sur la carte le temps qu'il fait en France.*

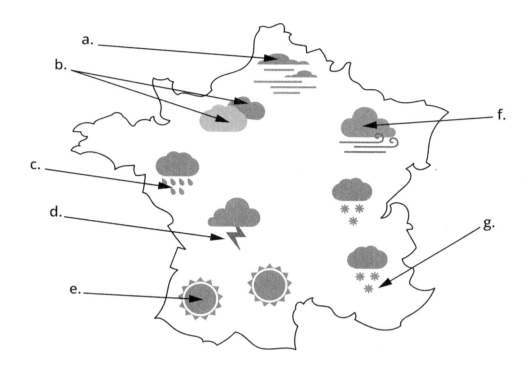

a. _____

b. _____

c. _____

d. _____

e. _____

f. _____

g. _____

INDEFINITES
LES INDÉFINIS

In this section, you are going to learn about les **indéfinis** (*indefinite*). First, we are going to start with **les adjectifs indéfinis** (*indefinite adjectives*). They are used to **describe** elements of a group or groups in their entirety. When we talk about an element, we talk about something or someone that is part of a group. Therefore, in what follows, when talking about an element, it can refer to a human being, an animal, an inanimate object or even something abstract and immaterial, like a thought.

Here is a list of indefinite adjectives:

a. **Quelques**
   some

b. **Plusieurs**
   several

c. **Chaque**
   each

d. **Tous** (plural, for masculine or mixed groups) **or toutes** (plural, for feminine groups).

e. **Tout** (masculine form) or **toute** (feminine form)
   the entire or the whole

f. **Certains** (masculine form) or **certaines** (feminine form)
   certain

g. **Aucun** (masculine form) or **aucune** (feminine form)
   none

Quelques is used to **describe** a **small number** of something.

For example:

a. **Quelques** pommes sont tombées de l'arbre ce matin.
   Some apples fell from the tree this morning.

Plusieurs is used to describe a **bigger** number of things than **quelques**.

For example:

    a. **Plusieurs** pommes sont tombées de l'arbre ce matin.
       Several apples fell from the tree this morning.

It means that **more** apples than **quelques** (*some*) fell from the tree.

Chaque is used to describe **every single element** of a group individually.

    a. **Chaque** membre du groupe a son propre livre.
       Each member of the group has their own book.

Tous or **toutes** is used to talk about **all** the elements of a group. The **"all the elements of a group"** concept is extremely important. This is because there are false friends within the language itself, where some words have the same spelling but do not refer to the same thing.

For example:

    a. Je mange des abricots **tous** les matins.
       I eat apricots every morning.

In this example, '**tous les**' is translated as **every**. To remember that you should use '**tous les**' in this kind of context, you should ask yourself whether you are talking about **all elements** of a group. '**Tous les matins**' means '**tous les matins de la semaine or de l'année**' (*every morning of the week or of the year*), or '**de la vie**' (*life*) in general. If all elements can fit in a higher group, then you should use '**tous**' or '**toutes**'. Then, there are easier examples where the word '**tous**' or '**toutes**' also translate as **all**.

Example with tous:

    a. **Tous les** chats (masculine and plural) du village m'aiment bien.
       All the village's cats like me.

    b. **Tous les** chats (masculine and plural) et les sauterelles (feminine and plural) sont des animaux.
       All cats and grasshoppers are animals.

As usual in French, if a group is composed of **both** masculine and feminine subjects, the adjective is in the **masculine plural form**, in this case **tous**.

Example with toutes:

    a. **Toutes** les chaises de la maison sont cassées.
       All the chairs of the house are broken.

"**Tout**" or "**toute**" is used to describe a group or set in its **entirety**.

    a. **Tout** le groupe a décidé de faire une pause.
       The whole group decided to have a break.

    b. **Toute** la famille s'est réunie pour regarder un film.
       The whole family decided to gather to watch a movie.

Usually, when you think about **whole** or **entire** in English, you can use '**tout**' or '**toute**' and their **plural** forms, '**tous**' and '**toutes**', respectively. Just remember to make it agree with the noun it precedes! And you remember '**tous**' les matins in the previous example above? It is the plural version of '**tout**'! That is why it is important to understand whether you are talking about **every** element of a set or group or if you are talking about the **group as a whole**. All these rules may seem confusing, but with exercises and then through practice in your daily life, by reading, speaking, and listening to French, you will gradually assimilate the concepts.

"**Certains**" (masculine) or "**certaines**" (feminine) is used to talk about a **part** of the group or set. In the most common use cases, it works in a very similar way as in English.

    a. **Certains** nombres sont premiers.
       Certain numbers are prime.

    b. **Certaines** tables sont en bois.
       Certain tables are made of wood.

You might be tempted to think that '**quelques**' (*some*) and '**certains**' or '**certaines**' (*certain*) are absolutely the same and serve the exact same function. From a linguistic perspective, this is not entirely true. As we mentioned, '**quelques**' (*some*) refers to a **small** amount whereas '**certains**' (*certain*) are only used to talk about a part of a bigger superset. This might not seem straightforward in daily speech. While this may not represent a hindrance in daily communication, being precise is part of our duties in this book. Besides, it is always important to understand and master the very basics to be able to build on solid foundations.

Finally, "**aucun**" is used to describe an element of a set or group that **does not exist**.

a. **Aucun** téléphone n'est fabriqué en Antarctique.
No phone is made in Antarctica.

b. **Aucune** fenêtre n'est ouverte.
No window is open.

c. Combien d'enfants jouent dans le parc ? **Aucun**.
How many children are playing in the park? None.

d. Combien de guitares sont cassées ? **Aucune**.
How many guitars are broken? None.

Please note that "**aucun**" cannot be used in conjunction with "**pas**". It is **either one or the other**.

a. Je **n'**ai **pas** d'ami vietnamien, malheureusement.
I do not have any Vietnamese friend, unfortunately.

b. Je **n'**ai **aucun** ami vietnamien, malheureusement.
I have no Vietnamese friend, unfortunately.

EXERCISES
EXERCICES

1. **Complete the sentences with one of the following indefinite adjectives: chacun, aucun, tous/toutes, quelques, plusieurs, certains.** *Complétez les phrases avec l'un des adjectifs indéfinis suivants : chacun, aucun, tous/toutes, quelques, plusieurs, certains.*

    a. _____ soir, j'achète du pain à la boulangerie.
    Every night, I buy some bread at the bakery.

    b. Je n'en ai _____ idée.
    I have no idea.

    c. J'ai _____ tomates dans le réfrigérateur.
    I have some tomatoes in the fridge.

    d. Lisa s'est inscrite à _____ cours.
    Lisa enlisted for several classes.

    e. _____ personnes préfèrent le beurre demi-sel.
    Some people prefer lightly salted butter.

    f. C'est un film pour _____.
    It's a movie for all.

TALKING ABOUT DURATION
LA DURÉE

We use different expressions to talk about duration, depending on the type of duration, whether it is over, still ongoing, a duration in the future, or in the past:

a. J'habite en France **depuis** 12 ans.
I have been living in France for 12 years.

b. J'ai vécu en France **pendant** 4 ans.
I have lived in France for 4 years.

c. On va en Italie **pour** les vacances.
We're going to Italy for the holidays.

d. Je l'ai croisée **il y a** trois jours.
I ran into her three days ago.

Depuis (*for/since*) followed by a duration expresses an ongoing duration, it has started in the past and continues today. It can only be used with the present:

a. Je pratique la danse **depuis** mes 8 ans.
I've been learning dancing since I was 8 years old (and still am).

Pendant (*for, while*) is used to refer to a duration that is over and has a clear beginning and a clear end:

a. Il t'a attendu **pendant** deux jours.
He has waited for you for two days. (but stopped)

Pour (*for*) is a preposition used to talk about a duration in the future, you announce that you're going to do something for a specific length of time:

a. Je peux t'emprunter ta voiture **pour** le weekend ?
Can I borrow your car for the weekend?

Finally, **il y a** (*ago*) expresses a duration in the past that is clearly defined:

a. J'ai déménagé **il y a** deux mois.
I moved out two months ago.

EXERCISES
EXERCICES

1. Listen and complete the sentences with the Expression of Duration: depuis, pendant, pour, il y a. *Écoutez et complétez les phrases avec l'expression de durée : depuis, pendant, pour, il y a.*

a. Je lis _____ trois heures.
I've been reading for three hours.

b. Je pars à Toulouse _____ trois jours.
I'm going to Toulouse for three days.

c. Chaque jour, je me promène _____ une heure.
Every day, I walk for one hour.

d. Elles sont amies _____ des années.
They've been friends for years.

e. J'ai lancé le four _____ vingt minutes.
I turned the oven on 20 minutes ago.

f. Elle a révisé _____ des jours pour cet examen.
She has crammed for days for this exam.

g. J'ai loué une voiture _____ la semaine.
I rented a car for the week.

h. Ce magasin existe _____ 1991.
This shop has existed since 1991.

i. J'ai vu ce film _____ longtemps.
I saw this movie a long time ago.

ADVERBS
LES ADVERBES

Adverbs are words that usually **answer the question "how."** They are similar to adjectives in that they modify another word; but contrary to adjectives, which modify nouns, adverbs modify verbs, adjectives, or other adverbs. In English, adverbs usually end in **-ly,** while in French they usually end in **-ment**.

For example:

    a. Il parle lente**ment**.
       He speaks slowly.

    b. Elles apprennent facile**ment**.
       They learn easily.

To form an adverb in French, you're going to take the adjective and then **change the ending of the word**:

Step 1: Take the feminine form of an adverb

Step 2: Add -ment at the end

a. lent   →   lent**e**   →   lente**ment** (*slowly*)

b. doux   →   dou**ce**   →   douce**ment** (*gently*)

This method works for most adverbs, but it wouldn't be French if it worked every time. Forming adverbs with adjectives **ending in -ant and -ent** is a bit different. The adjectives ending in **-ant** will be formed with **-amment** at the end and the adjectives ending in **-ent** will be formed with **-emment** at the end without using the feminine form of the adjective.

For example:

a. courant   →   cour**amment**

Elle parle français **couramment.**
She speaks French fluently.

b. violent   →   viol**emment**

La fenêtre a claqué **violemment.**
The window was slammed violently.

However, you cannot form all adverbs like this, there are exceptions to the general rule. Here are the **most frequent irregular adverbs:**

ADJECTIVE	ADVERB
Bon / *good*	Bien / *well*
Mauvais / *bad*	Mal / *badly*
Meilleur / *better*	Mieux / *better*
Moindre / *less*	Moins / *less*

a. Il parle **bien** français.
He speaks French well.

b. Elle s'est fait **mal.**
She hurt herself badly.

In a simple sentence, it is fairly easy to know **where to put your adverb**; it comes **after the verb** it modifies:

a. Elle dort **confortablement.**
She is sleeping comfortably.

b. Il lit **sérieusement.**
He is reading seriously.

However, an adverb can modify more than just the verb. **Sometimes, it modifies everything** that comes after the verb as well. The adverb will come **after everything it modifies**.

For example:

a. Ils jouent aux jeux-vidéos **bruyamment.**
They play video games loudly.

b. Elle a réussi ses examens **brillamment.**
She passed her exams brillantly.

Other times, the adverb **modifies a whole sentence**, so you can put it at the **very beginning of the sentence**:

a. Heureusement, ses clés étaient dans son sac à main.
Fortunately, her keys were in her handbag.

b. Soudainement, il s'est mis à hurler après sa sœur.
Suddenly, he started screaming at his sister.

EXERCISES
EXERCICES

1. Form adverbs with the adjectives given here. *Formez des adverbes avec les adjectifs suivants.*

    a. Rapide : _____

    b. Fort : _____

    c. Heureux : _____

    d. Certain : _____

    e. Constant : _____

    f. Silencieux : _____

    g. Évident : _____

2. Listen to the sentences and complete them with the right adverb. *Écoutez les phrases et complétez-les avec le bon adverbe.*

    a. Elle va _____ à la boulangerie.
    She rarely goes to the bakery.

    b. Il faut traverser la rue _____.
    You need to cross the street carefully.

    c. Les enfants lisent _____ dans le salon.
    The kids are reading silently in the living room.

    d. Tom comprend _____ le français.
    Tom understands French well.

    e. Ce costume te va _____.
    This suit suits you better.

    f. On se perd _____ dans les rues de Paris.
    You can easily get lost in the streets of Paris.

    g. Elle a parlé _____.
    She spoke frankly.

EXPRESSING QUANTITIES
LES QUANTITÉS

We use different expressions to talk about **quantities,** depending on whether they are **specified or unspecified**.

    a. Il y a **beaucoup** de soleil.
       There is a lot of sun. (unspecified)

    b. J'ai vu **trois** enfants jouer dans la rue.
       I saw three kids playing in the street. (specified)

We can use numbers, expressions, and adverbs for countable nouns but for uncountable nouns, we have to use partitive articles.

    a. Il a mis **du** temps à venir.
       He took his time coming here.

    b. Elle écoute **de la** musique.
       She listens to music.

SPECIFIED QUANTITIES
QUANTITÉS PRÉCISES

For **specified quantities**, we use **cardinal numbers**. They are invariable except "**un**" (**one**), which will agree with the gender of the noun it modifies.

    a. Nous avons **douze** œufs dans le réfrigérateur.
       We have twelve eggs in the fridge.

    b. Il y a **une** lampe sur la table.
       There is a lamp on the table. (lamp is feminine)

It only works with **countable nouns**. If you want to talk about a specified quantity of an **uncountable noun**, you will need to **use an expression** that will make it countable:

    a. Il nous faut deux **briques** de lait.   **b.** Il y a six **parts** de gâteau.
       We need two cartons of milk.   *There are six slices of cake.*

We also use **many expressions of quantity:** une tasse de / a cup of, un verre de / a glass of, une boîte de / a box of, une conserve de / a can of, un sac de / a bag of, un morceau de / a piece of, une douzaine de / a dozen of…

FOOD QUANTITIES

un morceau
de fromage

une part
de gâteau

une tablette
de chocolat

une douzaine
d'œufs

une tasse
de thé

une miche
de pain

un pot
de confiture

un régime
de bananes

un verre
d'eau

UNSPECIFIED QUANTITIES
QUANTITÉS IMPRÉCISES

For **unspecified quantities**, we use adverbs of quantity to give an idea of how much of it we are talking about even though we are not sure:

a. J'ai mis **trop de** carottes dans la soupe.
I put too many carrots in the soup.

b. Il y a **de** l'eau dans la bouteille.
There is water in the bottle.

There is an easy scale of **adverbs of quantity** that you can learn that will allow you to talk about **measures of quantity**:

peu / *little*	assez / *enough*	beaucoup / *a lot*	trop / *too much*

Adverbs of quantity are placed **before the noun** they modify:

a. Il a **trop de** <u>chaussures.</u>
He has too many pairs of shoes. (countable)

b. Il y a **peu de** <u>sel</u> dans ce plat.
There is little salt in this dish. (uncountable)

Remember to add "**de**" **after your adverb of quantity**. It is necessary before a noun.

Partitive articles are also used for unspecified quantities. As a quick reminder, the **masculine** partitive article is **du**, the **feminine** partitive article is **de la**, before a <u>noun starting with a vowel or a silent h</u> it will be **de l'**, and for a **plural** it will be **des.**

a. Il y a **du** chocolat
There is chocolate. (masculine, uncountable)

b. J'ai acheté **de la** raclette pour le dîner.
I bought some raclette for dinner. (feminine, countable)

c. Ils ont mangé **des** fraises à midi.

They had strawberries for lunch. (feminine, countable, plural)

d. Elle a **de l'**énergie le matin.

She is energetic in the morning. (feminine, uncountable)

With a negation, the partitive article becomes **de** for all nouns:

a. Il y a **du** café. => il n'y a pas **de** café.

There is coffee. => there is no coffee.

b. Elle a mangé **de la** salade. => elle n'a pas mangé **de** salade.

She had some salad => she didn't have any salad.

But don't forget to add an **-s** at the end for countable nouns used in the <u>plural form</u>:

a. Il n'y a plus **de** tomate**s**.

*There are **no** tomatoe**s** left.*

b. Il n'y a pas **de** taxi**s** dans la rue.

*There are **no** taxi**s** on the street.*

EXERCISES

EXERCICES

1. **Complete the following sentences with the right expression of quantity**. *Complétez les phrases suivantes en utilisant la bonne expression de quantité.*

   a. Il y a _____ lait, _____ œufs et _____ farine.

   There is milk, some eggs, and flour.

   b. Ils ont acheté _____ chaises, _____ table et _____ fauteuil.

   They bought four chairs, one table, and one armchair.

   c. Ils ont vendu _____ produits pendant la convention.

   They sold a lot of products during the convention.

   d. Maman prépare toujours _____ nourriture quand on vient dîner.

   Mom always cooks too much food when we come for dinner.

   e. Est-ce que vous voulez _____ ketchup ou _____ mayonnaise avec votre plat ?

   Would you like some ketchup or some mayonnaise with your meal?

   f. Il n'y a plus _____ croque-monsieur mais je peux vous proposer _____ steak avec _____ frites.

   We don't have any croque-monsieurs left, but we can serve you a steak with fries.

   g. On a fait _____ marche pour aujourd'hui.

   That's enough walking for today.

THE PRONOUN « EN »
LE PRONOM « EN »

The pronoun **en** is used to talk about previously mentioned things and places. It is very useful tool **to avoid repetition**, and we use it frequently in everyday French. **We use it regardless of the gender or number to which it refers.** You may find it difficult to understand at first because it is used in many different ways, but it will be a very useful pronoun for you and allow you to avoid repetition.

a. J'ai parlé **du problème** au patron.
I told the boss about the problem.

J'**en** ai parlé au patron.
I told the boss about it.

b. J'ai acheté **de la salade** pour ce soir.
I've bought some salad for tonight.

J'**en** ai acheté pour ce soir.
I've bought some for tonight.

Most of the time it is used to avoid repeating a (group) noun following a verb constructed with **de.** It can replace a (group) noun or an infinitive.

a. Je viens **de Bordeaux.**
I'm from Bordeaux.

J'**en** viens.
I'm from there.

b. J'ai parlé **d'aller au cinéma** avec Chantal.
I talked about going to the cinema with Chantal.

J'**en** ai parlé avec Chantal.
I've talked about it with Chantal.

It is also used to avoid repeating nouns introduced by a partitive like **du**, **de,** or an indefinite article like **un, une.** If you're talking about a precise quantity, you need to repeat that quantity in the sentence with **en** to keep it clear.

a. Tu veux **du poisson** ? Oui j'**en** veux.
Do you want some fish? Yes, I do.

b. Tu as **un smartphone** ? Oui, j'**en** ai <u>un</u>.
Do you have a smartphone? Yes, I do.

When you use **en**, you put it **right before the verb** even when there is a negation:

a. Elle veut **de la raclette** pour le dîner.
   She wants raclette for dinner.

   Elle **en** veut pour le dîner.
   She wants this for dinner.

b. Tu as entendu parler **du dernier film d'action au cinéma** ? Non, je n'**en** ai pas entendu parler.

   Did you hear about the latest action movie at the theatre? No, I haven't.

EXERCISES

EXERCICES

1. Answer the question using « en ». *Répondez à la question en utilisant « en ».*

a. Combien de sœurs as-tu ? _____

How many sisters do you have? I have two (of them).

b. Est-ce que tu manges des fruits ? _____

Do you eat fruit? Yes, I eat some (of it).

c. Est-ce qu'il y a des bus qui passent près de chez toi ? _____

Are there buses that drive near your house? Yes, there are some (of them).

d. Est-ce que le journaliste a parlé de ton école à la télé ? _____

Has the anchor talked about your school on TV? Yes, he talked about it.

e. Combien de boulangeries y a-t-il dans ton quartier ? _____

How many bakeries are there in your district? There are three.

f. Est-ce que tu as trouvé des vêtements qui te plaisaient ? _____

Did you find clothes you liked? Yes, I found some.

g. Tu veux une part de gâteau ? _____

Do you want a slice of cake? Yes, I want one

h. Il reste du lait ? _____

Is there any milk left? Yes, there is some left.

COMPARATIVE AND SUPERLATIVE
COMPARATIF ET SUPERLATIF

COMPARATIVE
LE COMPARATIF

We use slightly different expressions to make comparisons, depending on the nature of the word used to compare, whether it's an adjective, an adverb, a noun, or a verb. Here they are:

With an adjective	**Plus (+)** **Moins (-)** **Aussi (=)**	Adjective	**que**
With an adverb	**Plus (+)** **Moins (-)** **Aussi (=)**	Adverb	**que**
With a noun	**Plus de (+)** **Moins de (-)** **Autant de (=)**	Noun	**que**
With a verb	Verb	**plus (+)** **moins (-)** **autant (=)**	**que**

a. Cet appartement est **plus grand que** le mien.
This apartment is bigger than mine.

b. Je passe **moins de temps que toi** devant la télé.
I spend less time than you watching TV.

c. Il y a **autant de place que** dans le métro.
There is as much room as in the subway.

d. Ce magasin **vend plus que** celui d'à côté.
This shop sells more than the one next to it.

There are a few exceptions with some frequent adjectives and adverbs that have an <u>irregular form of comparative</u>: **bon** (*good*) and **mauvais** (*bad*) as well as **bien** (*well*); **bon(ne)** becomes **meilleur(e)**, **mauvais(e)** becomes **pire**, **bien** becomes **mieux**.

a. Ce restaurant est **meilleur que** celui d'hier.
This restaurant is better than the one from yesterday.

b. C'est **pire que** l'année dernière.
This is worse than last year.

c. Cette nouvelle employée travaille **mieux que** la précédente.
This new employee works better than the previous one.

SUPERLATIVE
LE SUPERLATIF

Superlatives are a form of comparison, but they express the idea that something is the best or the worst in something. As for comparatives, we use slightly different expressions depending on the nature of the word used.

With an adjective	Le plus (+) Le moins (-)	Adjective	(de)
With an adverb	Le plus (+) Le moins (-)	Adverb	(de)
With a noun	Le plus de (+) Le moins de (-)	Noun	que
With a verb	Verb	le plus (+) le moins (-)	que

a. Cet appartement est **le plus petit.**
This apartment is the smallest.

b. Il parle **le plus calmement** du monde.
He speaks in the calmest tone in the world.

c. C'est toi qui passes **le moins de temps** devant la télé.
You're the one who spends the least amount of time in front of the TV.

d. C'est elle qui travaille **le plus.**
She is the one who works the most.

Then again, there are some irregular superlatives with:

bon becomes **le/la meilleur(e)**
mauvais becomes **le/la pire**
bien becomes **le/la mieux**.

    a. Cette entreprise est **la meilleure !**
       This company is the best!

    b. C'est la **pire** journée de ma vie !
       This is the worst day of my life!

    c. Ce sont les fleurs qui se voient **le mieux !**
       These are the flowers you can see the best.

EXERCISES
EXERCICES

1. Complete the comparative sentence. *Complétez la phrase avec un comparatif.*

a. (+ petit) Laura est _____ Raphaël.
Laura is smaller than Raphael.

b. (- attentivement) Les enfants écoutent _____ leurs parents.
Kids listen less attentively than their parents.

c. (= long) Le trajet pour Paris est _____ pour Bordeaux.
The journey to Paris is as long as the one to Bordeaux.

d. (+ bon) Ce livre est _____ le film.
The book is better than the movie.

e. (- temps) Ce dossier prend _____ le précédent.
This case is taking less time than the previous one.

f. (= convient) Ce métier lui _____ le mien.
This job suits him as much as mine does.

2. Listen to each sentence carefully. Each sentence will have a missing superlative that you need to identify and provide. *Écoutez chaque phrase attentivement. Chaque phrase aura un superlatif manquant que vous devrez identifier et fournir.*

a. (- beau) C'est _____ tableau des trois.
It's the least beautiful painting out of the three.

b. (+ mauvais) Ce vin est _____ j'ai bu.
This is the worst wine I have ever had.

c. (+ bien) C'est ton livre qui avance _____.
Your book is the one that is progressing the best.

d. (- rapidement) C'est l'entreprise qui travaille _____.

It's the company that works the least quickly.

e. (+ éclaire) C'est la lampe qui _____.

This is the lamp that gives the most light.

f. (+ énergie) C'est Paula qui a _____.

Paula is the most energetic one.

THE VERB TO GO
LE VERBE ALLER

The verb "**aller**" means to go, it is used literally to mean **to go somewhere** but it is also used in a more figurative way to **indicate an intention to do something, or that something is going to happen;** a bit like "going to" in English, it is about actions. It can create some confusion at first, but you'll quickly get the hang of it and be able to use it yourself.

a. Je **vais** au cinema.
   I'm going to the cinema. (literal use)

b. Il **va** parler à mon frère.
   He's going to talk to my brother. (figurative use)

Here is the table of conjugation of aller in the **present tense**. It is a bit more varied than the English equivalent, but that's unsurprising with French:

Je vais	*I go*
Tu vas	*You go*
Il, elle va	*He, she, it goes*
Nous allons	*We go*
Vous allez	*You go*
Ils vont	*They go*

When "**aller**" is used **literally**, it is followed by a **preposition** introducing a place, such as "**à**", "**chez**", "**dans**":

a. Je <u>vais</u> **au** marché.
   I'm going to the market.

c. Vous <u>allez</u> **dans** le salon.
   You're going into the living room.

b. Ils <u>vont</u> **chez** leur tante.
   They're going to their aunt's.

When you use **aller** to talk about a place, you're going to use the preposition "**à**"; if the place is *masculine,* you're going to use "**au**" (à + le); and if the place is a *plural,* you're going to use "**aux**" (à + les) as your preposition:

a. Je **vais au** théâtre.
   I'm going to the theatre.

b. Nous **allons aux** galeries d'art.
   We're going to the art galleries.

When we use it **figuratively,** "**aller**" is followed by a **verb in the infinitive form**, indicating what the intention is. "**Aller**" indicates the intention, the verb that follows indicates what the intention is:

a. Je **vais** <u>prendre</u> le métro.
   I'm going to take the subway.

b. Elle **va** <u>demander</u> à un joueur.
   I'm going to ask a player.

EXERCISES

EXERCICES

1. **Complete the sentences**. *Complétez les phrases.*

    a. Je _____ le fleuriste.
    I'm going to the florists.

    b. Tu _____ ton oncle.
    You're going to ask your uncle.

    c. Elle _____ le médecin.
    She's going to the doctors.

    d. Nous _____ la situation.
    We're going to talk about the situation.

    e. Vous _____ ce livre.
    You're going to like this book.

    f. Ils _____ la salle de sport.
    They are going to the gym.

2. **Answer the following questions with the elements given**. *Répondez aux questions suivantes avec les éléments donnés.*

    a. Où allez-vous ? (piscine)
    Where are you going? (swimming pool)

    _____

    b. Que va faire Thomas après le lycée ? (étudier le droit)
    What is Thomas going to do after high school? (study law)

    _____

    c. Que vont faire les enfants le samedi soir ? (voir un film)
    What are the kids going to do on Saturday night? (watch a movie)

    _____

d. Que va faire le président ? (faire un discours)

What is the president going to do? (give a speech)

_____

e. Qu'est-ce que tu vas faire pour l'anniversaire de papa ? (inviter tout le monde au restaurant)

What are you going to do for dad's birthday? (invite everyone to the restaurant)

_____

THE PRONOUN « Y »
LE PRONOM « Y »

The pronoun "**y**" is an adverbial pronoun that is **used to refer to places or things previously mentioned or identified**. It is never used to refer to people. It is a very useful word to avoid repetition and it is very frequently used in everyday French. It is **pronounced like the letter** "i" **in French**, and it is considered like a vowel sound so you will need to do liaison.

For example:

    a. Tu es allé **au cinéma** hier ? Oui, j'**y** suis allée.
       Did you go to the cinema yesterday? Yes, I did.

    b. Ils ont pensé à **organiser Noël** ? Oui, ils **y** ont pensé.
       Did they remember to organize Christmas Eve? Yes, they did.

When **it refers to a place**, this pronoun often **means there**. It usually replaces a previously mentioned place introduced by the preposition "**à**" or other prepositions of place like "**dans**", "**derrière**", "**chez**", "**devant**", "**sur**"...

    a. Vous êtes allés **chez vos amis** ? Oui, nous **y** avons dîné.
       Did you go to your friends'? Yes, we had dinner there.

    b. Il travaille **dans ce magasin** depuis longtemps ? Non, il **y** travaille depuis deux mois.
       Has he been working in this shop for long? No, he's been working here for two months.

It is also **used to refer to things** when they **follow a verb that requires** "à" **and an indirect object** after it:

    a. Il va réussir **à finir sa thèse** ? Il **y** travaille.
       Will he manage to finish his PhD? He's working on it.

    b. Elle a décidé de répondre "**à sa lettre**". – Elle va vraiment **y** répondre ?
       She decided to answer his letter. – Is she really going to answer it?

When it refers to something, "**y**" can also be used to refer to an entire phrase, clause or idea:

a. **Il y a beaucoup de règles de grammaire en français.** Il faut **y** faire attention.
There are many rules in French grammar, you need to pay attention to that.

b. **Il y a un nouveau café en ville.** Nous devons **y** aller.
There is a new café in town. We should go there.

Like **en,** it comes immediately **before the verb**, even when there is a negation:

a. Tu as aimé **l'exposition** ? – Je n'**y** suis pas allée.
Did you enjoy the exhibition? – I didn't go.

EXERCISES
EXERCICES

1. **Rewrite the sentence using "y"**. *Réécrivez la phrase en utilisant « y ».*

   a. Le chat dort sur le canapé toute la journée.   _____.

   The cat sleeps on the couch all day.   *The cat sleeps there all day.*

   b. Paul adore jouer dans le parc.   _____

   Paul loves playing in the park.   *Paul loves playing there.*

   c. Lucile est à la banque derrière la boulangerie.   _____

   Lucile is at the bank behind the bakery.   *Lucile is there.*

   d. Cédric pense à déménager en Guadeloupe.   _____

   Cedric is thinking of moving to Guadeloupe.   *Cedric is thinking of moving there.*

2. **Answer the question using "y"**. *Répondez à la question en utilisant « y ».*

   a. Vous allez au parc ?
   Are you going to the park?

   Oui, _____.
   Yes, we are going there.

   b. Marie pense à ses vacances ?
   Is Marie thinking about her vacation?

   Oui, _____.
   Yes, she is thinking about it.

   c. Tu vas au supermarché ?
   Are you going to the supermarket?

   Oui, _____.
   Yes, I am going there.

d. Nous réfléchissons à notre projet ?

Are we thinking about our project?

Oui, _____.

Yes, we are thinking about it.

COMPLEMENT PRONOUNS
LES PRONOMS COMPLÉMENTS

Complement pronouns are pronouns that are used **after a verb**, they complement the sentence by referring to a person, an animal or something to avoid repetition. They are **used with verbs that take a direct or indirect object**.

a. Elle **le** lit.
She's reading it. (direct object)

b. Il **me** parle.
He's talking to me. (indirect object, i.e., introduced by a preposition)

DIRECT OBJECT PRONOUNS
PRONOMS COMPLÉMENTS D'OBJET DIRECT

Me /m'	*Me*
Te /t'	*You*
Le / l' La / l'	*Him / it* *Her / it*
Nous	*Us*
Vous	*You*
Les	*Them*

The above table provides all of the direct object pronouns. We use direct object pronouns with **verbs that take a direct object** to avoid repeating the noun we used previously.

The direct object pronoun is generally placed **before the verb**:

a. Il **la** lave. (la vaisselle)
He's doing it. (the dishes)

b. Elle **l'**aime. (le chien)
She likes him. (the dog)

The pronouns

me / me,
te / you,
le / him
and **la / her**
become **m', t', l'** when **the verb that follows starts with a vowel.**

For example:

    a. Ils **l'**apportent demain.
        They are bringing it tomorrow.

    b. Nous **t'**appellerons la semaine prochaine.
        We'll call you next week.

INDIRECT OBJECT PRONOUNS
PRONOMS COMPLÉMENTS D'OBJET INDIRECT

We use indirect object pronouns with **verbs** that are **constructed with a preposition** when we use the full noun and not a pronoun:

    a. Vous parlez **à Paula.** => Vous **lui** parlez.
        You're talking to Paula. => You're talking to her.

    b. Je montre mon travail **à mes parents.** => Je **leur** montre mon travail.
        I'm showing my work to my parents. => I'm showing my work to them.

The list of pronouns is slightly different from the direct object pronouns (see pronouns in bold). Here it is:

Me / m'	*To / for me*
Te / t'	*To / for you*
Lui	***To/for her, him, it***
Nous	*To / for us*
Vous	*To / for you*
Leur	***To / for them***

a. Mon frère **leur** achète des jouets. (aux enfants)
*My brother buys **them** toys. (to the kids)*

b. Vous ne **lui** écrivez pas. (à Laura)
*You don't write **to her**. (Laura)*

In French, indirect object pronouns are **only used to refer to people** or other animate nouns like animals. For other inanimate nouns, you will use the adverbial pronoun **y**. The indirect object pronoun usually answers the question *to whom?* **or** *for whom?* The pronoun usually comes **before the verb**.

For example:

a. Je **te** parle souvent.
I often talk to you.

b. Laurent **nous** a préparé le dîner.
Laurent made us dinner. (for us)

c. J'**y** réponds. (ton e-mail)
I'm answering it. (your email)

Be careful, **from one language to the next, verbs are not constructed the same**. Some English verbs may not take an object while the equivalent in French does and vice versa.

For example:

a. Je rends visite <u>à ma tante.</u> => Je **lui** rends visite.
I'm visiting <u>my aunt.</u> => I'm visiting her.

b. Tu **m'**as téléphoné. (téléphoner à)
You called me. (on the phone)

DOUBLE OBJECT PRONOUNS
DOUBLE COMPLÉMENTS D'OBJET

Some verbs take two objects, a direct object pronoun and an indirect object pronoun, so the simple question here is what is the order? Here is how it works: "**me**", "**te**", "**se**", "**nous**", or "**vous**" come before "**le**", "**la**", "**l'**", or "**les**", which come *before* "**lui**" or "**leur**" which come before "**y**", which comes before "**en**".

For example:

a. Il **me la** montre. (sa montre)
*He's showing **it to me** (his watch).*

b. Tu **nous en** donnes. (des nouvelles)
*You give **us some** (news).*

c. Ne **vous** l'envoyez pas. (la lettre)
*Don't send **it to yourself**. (the letter)*

Here is an image to help you remember it better:

EXERCISES
EXERCICES

 **1. Listen to the sentences and complete them with the object pronouns**. *Écoutez les phrases et complétez-les avec un pronom complément.*

a. Je _____ invite à dîner.
I'm inviting him for dinner.

b. Nous _____ présentons à nos amis.
We are introducing them to our friends.

c. Je _____ montre mon salon demain.
I'll show you my living room tomorrow.

d. Tu _____ as dit ?
Did you tell him?

e. Elles _____ téléphoné pour _____ parler.
They called me to tell me about it.

2. Answer the following questions using a complement pronoun. *Répondez aux questions en utilisant un pronom complément.*

a. Vous aimez le film ?
Do you like the movie?

c. Ce jeu appartient à nos cousins ?
Does this game belong to our cousins?

_____

_____

b. Tu as parlé à Jeanne ?
Did you talk to Jeanne?

d. Ils vous ont croisé dans la rue ?
Did they run into you on the street?

_____

_____

STRESSED OR DISJUNCTIVE PRONOUNS
LES PRONOMS TONIQUES

Stressed pronouns are used to put an **extra emphasis on a subject or an object pronoun**. In English, you would emphasize it with your tone. They are very similar to object pronouns.

a. Mon frère à 35 ans, <u>elle</u>, elle en a 40.
My brother is 35, but she is 40.

b. Je ne le supporte pas, <u>lui</u>.
I can't stand him.

SUBJECT PRONOUNS	STRESSED PRONOUNS
Je / *I*	Moi / *me*
Tu / *you*	Toi / *you*
Il / *he* Elle / *she*	Lui / *him* Elle / *her*
Nous / *we*	Nous / *us*
Vous / *you*	Vous / *you*
Ils / *they* Elles / *they (all female)*	Eux / *them* Elles (all female) / *them*

We use it to put extra emphasis on someone, to single them out or attract their attention.

For example:

a. Toi, viens m'aider !
You, come help me!

b. Ils ont bien une deuxième voiture, **eux** !
They do have a second car!

Or we use it for <u>very simple sentences</u> with no verb or after "**c'est**" and "**ce sont**":

a. Toi et **moi**.
You and I.

b. C'est **nous** qui venons.
We are the ones coming.

Or for single word replies:

a. Qui veut du pain ? **Moi** !
Who wants bread? I do!

b. Qui est votre ami ? **Lui**.
Who is your friend? Him.

EXERCISES
EXERCICES

1. **Complete the sentences with the right stressed pronoun**. *Complétez les phrases avec le bon pronom tonique.*

    a. J'ai soif, et _____ ?
    I'm thirsty, what about you?

    b. J'étais à l'heure, _____.
    I was on time.

    c. C'est _____ qui organise le voyage ? Non, c'est _____.
    Does she organize the trip? –No, he does.

    d. Quelqu'un a vu mon téléphone ? _____.
    Has someone seen my phone? –She has.

    e. Nous sommes plus grands qu' _____.
    We are taller than them.

    f. Ce chien est à _____ ? Non, il est à _____.
    Is this dog yours (formal/plural)? –No, it's theirs (feminine).

RELATIVE PRONOUNS
LES RELATIVES

Relative pronouns are used to **connect two clauses** when there is a **common topic**. The relative clause allows you to **add more information** about that which you are talking, it also **avoids repetition** of the topic of conversation. The relative pronoun **connects the word right before** itself, called the antecedent, with the new part of the sentence. Contrary to English where you can often drop the "that," you can never drop relative pronouns in French.

For example:

    a. C'est la femme **qui** est venue hier. (both about: la femme)
    It's the woman who came yesterday.

    b. Le livre **que** j'ai lu était très intéressant. (both about: le livre)
    The book (that) I read was interesting.

    We only have a few relative pronouns. **Qui** is the most common. You can use **qui** for either people or things, which might be a bit odd for you as an English speaker. It can mean *who, which,* or *that:*

    a. J'ai vu le lit **qui** était dans la chambre.
    I saw the bed that was in the bedroom.

    b. C'est un jeune homme **qui** a travaillé pour ton oncle.
    It's a young man who worked for your uncle.

    There is also **preposition + qui,** which replaces a person and never an object because it means *whom*. You can have different prepositions right before the relative pronoun, such as "**à**", "**avec**", "**chez**"...

    a. L'ami **chez qui** je suis allé, m'a montré son jardin.
    The friend whom/that I visited showed me his garden.

    b. Les gens **avec qui** elle travaille sont sympathiques.
    The people with whom she works are friendly.

We also have "**que**" that is always used as a **direct object to a verb.** This means that the antecedent, the word right before the relative pronoun, is the direct object of the verb in your sentence. To check whether it's an object or subject of the verb, imagine the answer. If the element you're talking about comes after the verb in the answer, then it's an object. "**Que**" can mean *whom, which,* or *that.* As usual, "**que**" becomes "**qu'**" **before a vowel or a silent h**".

For example:

    a. Le poulet **que** tu as ramené était bon. (tu as ramené <u>du poulet</u>)
        The chicken (that) you brought was good. (you brought <u>the chicken</u>)

    b. Le cadeau **qu'**il demande est un peu cher. (il demande <u>un cadeau</u>)
        The gift (that) he is asking for is a bit expensive. (he's asking for <u>a gift</u>)

When we want to add more information about the place or the time about which we are talking, we are going to use **où / where**:

    a. C'est le moment **où** j'ai réalisé ma chance.
        That's when I realized how lucky I am.

    b. C'est le restaurant **où** nous avons déjeuné la semaine dernière.
        This is the restaurant where we had lunch last week.

Finally, there is **dont**, which is used when the antecedent is an object constructed with the preposition "**de**", such as:

avoir besoin de / to need to,
avoir envie de / to feel like,
avoir peur de / to be scared of...

    a. C'est le temps **dont** j'ai besoin pour finir ce travail. (j'ai besoin **de temps**)
        That's the time (that) I need to finish the job. (I need time)

    b. Le seul groupe **dont** je suis fan, c'est Les Beatles.
        The only band (that) I'm a fan of are The Beatles.

EXERCISES
EXERCICES

  1. Listen to the sentences and choose the right relative pronoun to complete the sentences. *Écoutez les phrases et choisissez le bon pronom relatif pour les phrases suivantes.*

a. C'est le plat _____ tu préfères.
It's your favorite meal.

b. Tu as lu le roman _____ vient de sortir ?
Have you read the novel that just came out?

c. J'ai appris _____ tu partais, c'est vrai ?
I heard you were quitting, is that true?

d. Du chocolat, voilà ce _____ j'ai envie.
Chocolate, that's what I feel like having.

e. Nous sommes allés là _____ nous nous sommes rencontrés.
We went back to where we first met.

f. Le médecin _____ tu parles, a fait des recherches sur le cancer.
The doctor with whom you're talking has done research on cancer.

2. **Listen to the sentences and choose the right relative pronoun to complete the sentences.**

    Écoutez les phrases et choisissez le bon pronom relatif pour les phrases suivantes.

    Example:

    *C'est un avocat. Il a 42 ans. Il vient de Chicago. → C'est un avocat **qui** a 42 ans et **qui** vient de Chicago.*

    *He's a lawyer. He's 42. He comes from Chicago. → It's a lawyer **who** is 42 and **who** comes from Chicago.*

    a. C'est un arbre. Il est grand. Il est vert.
    It's a tree. It's tall. It's green.

    _____

    b. Voici une maison. Je veux l'acheter. Elle me plaît.
    Here is a house. I want to buy it. I like it.

    _____

    c. J'ai déménagé en 2018. À ce moment-là, j'étais fleuriste.
    I moved in 2018. Back then, I was a florist.

    _____

    d. J'ai croisé un voisin. Il m'a parlé du barbecue de la semaine prochaine. Je ne m'en souvenais pas (*se souvenir de*).
    I ran into a neighbor. He told me about the barbecue next week. I didn't remember about it.

    _____

    e. C'est une salle de sport. J'y vais tous les vendredis. Elle est un peu chère.
    It's a gym. I go there every Friday. It's a bit expensive.

    _____

INTERROGATION
INTERROGATION

In chapter 9, we talked about simple questions or closed questions to which you answer yes or no. But there are also **open questions** to which you answer whatever you want. Those questions use <u>interrogative words</u>, Wh- words in English, to ask a more complex question. Here are the interrogative words in French:

Quoi / Que *(at the beginning of questions)*	*What*
Qui	*Who*
Quand	*When*
Où	*Where*
Pourquoi	*Why*
Comment	*How*
Combien	*How many/much*
Quel /Quelle / Lequel / Laquelle / Lesquels	*Which*

a. Qu'est-ce que tu fais aujourd'hui ?
What are you doing today?

b. Qui est là ?
Who is there?

c. Pourquoi êtes-vous venues ?
Why did you come?

There are **different ways to ask open questions** in French, depending on the situation or the people to whom you are talking. There is the simplest way, which is to **use a statement but raising your voice at the end to turn it into a question**. It works for yes/no questions and also for open questions:

a. Tu viens en bus demain ?
Are you coming by bus tomorrow?

b. Elle a vu ta sœur ce matin ?
Did she see you sister this morning?

The most colloquial form of questions can be used with friends and family and colleagues you know well. It works as follows:

Subject + verb + interrogative verb + (complement) + ?

a. Vous êtes là pour **quoi** ?
Why are you here?

b. Vous en voulez **combien** ?
How many do you want?

There is, then, the neutral form of questions that you can ask anybody without risk of sounding impolite, which works as follows:

Interrogative word + « est-ce que » + subject + verb + (complement) + ?

a. Quand est-ce que vous avez acheté votre maison ?
When did you buy your house?

b. Quel parc est-ce que tu préfères ?
Which park do you prefer?

Finally, on a very formal register, you would use the neutral form and add an inversion of the subject and the verb. It is used in formal conversations or settings. You won't need it much, but you will be able to recognize it:

Interrogative word + verb + subject + (complement) + ?

a. Que dites-vous ?
What are you saying?

b. Comment s'appelle-**t**-elle ?
What is she called?

When you have a verb that ends in a vowel followed by a subject that starts with a vowel, we add a "t" to make pronunciation easier.

EXERCISES
EXERCICES

1. **Complete the dialogue by rewriting the questions based on the answers**. *Complétez le dialogue en retrouvant les questions à partir des réponses.*

> **Example :** Pourquoi apprenez-vous le français ?
> *Why are you learning French?*
>
> J'apprends le français pour visiter la France.
> *I'm learning French to go visit France.*

    a. (formal) _____ ?
    What's his name?

    Il s'appelle Jean.
    His name is Jean.

    b. (informal) _____ ?
    Where are they going?

    Ils vont à l'école.
    They are going to school.

    c. (formal) _____ ?
    What are you doing here?

    Nous avons rendez-vous avec le président.
    We have an appointment with the president.

    d. (neutral) _____ ?
    How do you go to work?

    Je vais au travail en voiture.
    I drive to work.

    e. (informal) _____ ?
    What are you thinking about?

    Je pense à ma prochaine lecture.
    I'm thinking about the next book I'm going to read.

NEGATION – ADVANCED
NÉGATION – AVANCÉ

Moi, je n'aime pas la NÉGATION !

We touched on negation in Chapter 9.1 and explained that the simple form of negation is "**ne... pas**"; however, there are many more constructions that you can use. "**Ne**" doesn't change, it's the word coming after the verb that will vary:

a. Je **ne** mange **plus** de viande.
I don't eat meat anymore.

b. Ce bus **ne** va **nulle part**.
This bus isn't going anywhere.

c. Vous **n'**aimez **pas du tout** cet artiste.
You don't like this artist at all.

d. Mon cousin **n'**est **jamais** à l'heure.
My cousin is never on time.

The word "**sans**" (*without*) is another way to use negation, but it creates a few changes in the sentence. There is no article between "**sans**" and the word that follows but you keep possessive adjectives:

a. Il travaille avec des écouteurs.
He works with earphones on.
→ *Il travaille **sans** écouteurs.*
He works without earphones on.

b. Ton oncle est parti avec son sac.
Your uncle left with his bag.
→ *Ton oncle est parti **sans son** sac.*
Your uncle left without his bag.

If you want to use <u>negation for several elements</u>, you're going to use **ne ... ni... ni...**The articles also disappear when you use this expression:

a. La maison est grande, belle et moderne.
The house is big, beautiful and modern.
→ *La maison **n'**est **ni** grande, **ni** belle, **ni** moderne.*
The house is neither big, nor beautiful, nor modern.

b. Vous avez du ketchup ou de la mayonnaise ?
Do you have ketchup or mayonnaise?
→ *Nous n'avons **ni** ketchup **ni** mayonnaise.*
We have neither ketchup nor mayonnaise.

The last construction that will be useful to you for now, as you learn French, is the expression **ne ... que,** which is not a complete negation but simply restricts the scope of what you're talking about, but it's not necessarily meant as negative:

a. Je **n'**ai **que** dix minutes pour me préparer.
I only have ten minutes to get ready.

b. Il **ne** lui a fallu **que** deux œufs pour préparer ce gâteau.
She only used two eggs to make this cake.

EXERCISES
EXERCICES

1. Turn all the sentences in this short text into negative forms. *Transformez toutes les phrases à la forme négative.*

La famille Dupont vit dans une grande maison. Ils ont un chien et un chat. Il y a deux enfants. L'aîné, Victor, vit encore chez ses parents pendant ses études. La cadette, Laura, aime jouer au football. Constance, la mère, travaille avec son ordinateur à la maison. Léni, le père, passe ses journées au bureau. Il y va à vélo ou à pied.

The Duponts live in a big house. They have a dog and a cat. There are two kids. The oldest, Victor, still lives with his parents while he goes to university. The youngest, Laura, loves playing football. Constance, the mom, works from home with her computer. Léni, the father, spends his days at the office. He cycles or walks there.

_____

_____

_____

_____

_____

_____

_____

_____

INDIRECT SPEECH IN THE PRESENT TENSE
LE DISCOURS INDIRECT AU PRÉSENT

Indirect speech in the present tense is used to <u>report on what somebody said</u> using a verb of speech to introduce it. It is indirect because you don't say "I quote," but you rephrase the sentence with a verb of speech like "**dire**" (*say)*, "**demander**" (*ask)*, "**rappeler**" (*remind)*, etc.

For example:

    a. Mélanie **dit que** tu viens dîner.
       Mélanie says you're coming for dinner.

    b. Léopold **demande si** on aime la raclette.
       Léopold is asking if we like raclette.

Apart from using a verb of speech to introduce the reported speech, you also need <u>to change some pronouns</u> in the indirect speech. The original sentences that Mélanie or Léopold said included different pronouns because they were speaking directly:

    a. Mélanie : « **Il** vient dîner »
       *Mélanie: « **He**'s coming for dinner. »*

    b. Léopold : « **Vous** aimez la raclette ? »
       *Léopold: « Do **you** like raclette? »*

But it has to <u>change according to who you're reporting it to.</u>

a. Mélanie **dit que** <u>tu</u> viens dîner.

Mélanie says <u>you're</u> coming for dinner.

→ *If I'm talking to the person she was talking about. Let's say he's called Paul.*

b. Mélanie dit que **Paul/il** vient dîner

*Mélanie says **Paul/he** is coming for dinner.*

→ *If I'm talking to someone other than Paul.*

Depending on what you are reporting, you will use a different word between the verb of speech and what you are reporting, either a conjunction "**que**", "**si**", "**ce qui**", "**ce que**", or an interrogative pronoun:

Affirmation Je suis occupée. / *I'm busy.*	Verb of speech **+ que/qu'/** *that* Elle dit **qu'**elle est occupée. / *She says she is busy.*
Yes/no question Ils viennent dimanche ? / *Are they coming on Sunday?*	Verb of speech **+ si /** *if* Il demande s'ils viennent dimanche. / *He asks if they are coming on Sunday.*
Open question Vous repartez **quand** ? / *When are you leaving?*	Verb of speech **+ interrogative pronoun used** Tu demandes **quand** ils repartent. / *You're asking when they are leaving.*
Question with quoi, qu' / what Qu'est-ce que tu veux manger ? / *What do you want to eat?* Qu'est-ce qui te ferait plaisir pour Noël ? / ***What** would you like for Christmas?*	Verb of speech **+ ce qui (subject)/que (object)** Nous demandons **ce que** tu veux manger. / *We are asking **what** you want to eat. (object*)* Nous demandons **ce qui** te ferait plaisir pour Noël / *We are asking **what** you would like for Christmas. (subject**)*

* object because the answer is "je veux manger **X**" / *"I want to eat **X**"*

** subject because the answer is « **X** me ferait plaisir » / *"I would like **X**"*

 **EXERCISES**
EXERCICES

1. **Complete the sentences with the element missing: it can be the verb of speech, the word to connect the two sentences, or the pronouns**. *Complétez les phrases avec l'élément manquant, cela peut-être le verbe de parole, le mot connecteur ou les pronoms.*

   a. Lola : « Pourquoi vous déménagez ? »
   Lola: "Why are you moving?"

   Lola demande pourquoi _____ déménageons.
   Lola is asking why we are moving.

   b. Thomas : « Il y a beaucoup de boulangeries en France »
   Thomas: "There are a lot of bakeries in France."

   Thomas dit _____ il y a beaucoup de boulangeries en France.
   Thomas says that there are a lot of bakeries in France.

   c. Les Français : « Nous ne mangeons pas trop de pain. »
   French people: "We do not eat too much bread."

   Les Françaises disent _____ qu' _____ ne mangent pas trop de pain.
   French people say that they do not eat too much bread.

   d. Les Françaises : « Nous aimons marcher »
   French women: "We like to walk."

   Les Françaises disent _____ _____ aiment marcher.
   French women are saying that they like to walk.

2. **Transform the sentences in direct speech into sentences in indirect speech**.
   Transformez les phrases au discours direct en phrases au discours indirect.

   a. Amélia : « Viens t'asseoir à côté de moi »
   Amélia: "Come sit next to me. "

   _____

b. Les enfants : « Nous ne voulons pas aller nous coucher ».
The kids: "We don't want to go to bed."

_____

c. Timothé : « Vous allez souvent à la salle de sport ? »
Timothé: "Do you often go to the gym?"

_____

d. Moi : « Tu vas à Paris la semaine prochaine ? »
Me: "Are you going to Paris next week?"

_____

e. Toi : « Je n'aime pas les tomates. »
You: "I don't like tomatoes."

_____

PREPOSITIONS
LES PRÉPOSITIONS

Prepositions are invariable words that link two words together to give more information about the first word. It can introduce information about **the place, the time, the means of transportation, the direction,** etc. Here are the main prepositions in French:

Prepositions of place:

- **à** / at,
- **chez** / at,
- **dans** / in,

- **derrière** / behind,
- **devant** / in front of,
- **entre** / between,

- **sous** / under,
- **sur** / on

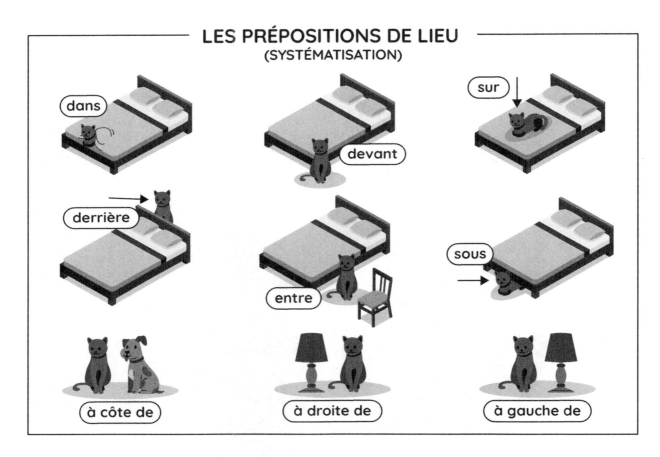

LES PRÉPOSITIONS DE LIEU
(SYSTÉMATISATION)

dans — devant — sur — derrière — entre — sous — à côté de — à droite de — à gauche de

a. Je suis **chez** ma sœur.
I am at my sister's.

b. Le chat est **derrière** le lit.
The cat is behind the bed.

Prepositions of time:

- **à** / at,
- **vers** / around,
- **en** / in,
- **après** / after,
- **dès** / as soon as,
- **pour** / for,
- **avant** / before,
- **pendant** / while,
- **durant** / during
- **depuis** / since,
- **dans** / in,

a. Je pars **à** dix heures.
*I'm leaving **at** ten.*

b. Je rentre **avant** le dîner.
*I'll be home **before** dinner.*

c. Vous mangerez **dès** que vous arriverez.
*You'll eat **as soon as** you arrive.*

Prepositions before means of transportation: "**en**" for shared means of transportation, "**à**" for individual means of transportation.

a. J'y vais **à** pied, **à** vélo, **à** moto...
I'm going on foot, by bicycle, by bike...

b. J'y vais **en** train, **en** avion, **en** bus, **en** voiture...
I'm going by train, by plane, by bus, by car...

Preposition of direction:

- **à** / to,
- **vers** / toward,
- **de** / from.

a. Je vais **à** l'école, **au** (à + le) bureau...
*I'm going **to** school, **to** the office...*

b. Je vais **vers** le centre-ville.
*I'm going **toward** the city center.*

c. Je rentre **de** la salle de sport, **du** (de + le) travail.
*I'm returning **from** the gym, **from** work.*

1. Write a sentence for each number indicating where the cat, mouse, or dog is.

Écrivez une phrase pour chaque numéro en indiquant où se trouve le chat, le chien ou la souris.

Example:

1. Le chat est sur le mur.
The cat is on the wall.

2. _____

3. _____

4. _____

5. _____

6. _____

7. _____

8. _____

9. _____

10. _____

2. **Complete the sentences with the right preposition**. *Complétez les phrases avec la bonne préposition.*

    a. Je vais _____ la piscine.
    I'm going to the swimming pool.

    b. Je rentre _____ stade.
    I'm returning from the stadium.

    c. Je vais _____ la boulangerie.
    I'm going toward the bakery.

    d. Je rentre à la maison _____ bus.
    I'm taking the bus home.

    e. Je vais chez mon ami _____ pied.
    I'm walking to my friend's house.

    f. J'ai réparé la voiture _____ que tu dormais.
    I fixed the car while you were sleeping.

THE PASSIVE VOICE
LE PASSIF

In French, as in English, there are two ways to express a sentence: the active voice where the subject of the sentence is doing the action of the verb or the **passive voice where the subject of the sentence is not the one doing the action.**

For example:

    a. <u>Active voice</u>: Le chat mange la souris.
       The cat is eating the mouse.

    b. <u>Passive voice</u>: La souris est mangée par le chat.
       The mouse is being eaten by the cat.

We use it when **the subject cannot be the one doing the action**, like a place, a thing, or an idea, but **we want to talk about that place, thing, or idea** and not who does the action. The **passive voice** can be used in **any grammatical tense**, it has no impact on when the action took place. The construction of a passive voice is similar to English:

Subject + être (conjugated) + past participle of the verb (+ par + agent)

As in English, **the agent**, the one who is actually doing the action, is **not always mentioned** if it isn't necessary, known, or deemed relevant.

    a. Le plat <u>est preparé</u> par le chef.
       The meal is prepared by the chef.

    b. Notre responsable <u>est envoyée</u> à Toulouse pour une conférence.
       Our manager is sent to Toulouse for a conference.

However, the **passive voice isn't used as frequently in French** as it is in English. It sounds a bit **formal** when there are other **simpler options** such as the third person singular pronoun "**on**". It doesn't refer to anyone specific, it is a general "**on**".

a. On m'a prévenu que tu venais.
I was told that you were coming. (it isn't felt relevant to say who)

b. On parle français ici.
French is spoken here. (the staff in the restaurant, for example)

The passive voice is also often **used to emphasize the object of the action** and not the subject. To do that, you can use the expression "**c'est**" or "**ce sont**" and avoid a rather formal passive voice.

a. C'est <u>Tom</u> que ma mère a emmené à la gare.
<u>*Tom*</u> ***was taken*** *to the train station by my mother.*

b. C'est <u>ta lettre</u> qui a été envoyée chez les Dupont.
<u>*Your letter*</u> ***was sent*** *to the Duponts.*

The **last possible option** to avoid using a passive voice is to use **a reflexive verb**, **se + verb**, to talk about things in general.

For example:

a. Le bon pain <u>se vendent</u> en boulangerie.
Good bread is sold in bakeries.

b. Elle <u>s'appelle</u> Aurélie.
She is called Aurélie.

EXERCISES
EXERCICES

1. **Transform the sentence in the active voice into a sentence in the passive voice. (You will only need the present tense of "être" to do it and the past participle of the verb in the sentence).** *Transformez la phrase à la voix active en phrase à la voix passive (vous n'avez besoin que du présent du verbe être et du participe passé du verbe).*

Example:

*Les élèves **apprécient** leur professeur.*　　　*Le professeur **est apprécié** des élèves.*

*The students **like** their teacher.*　　　*The teacher **is liked** by his students.*

a. Les ouvriers construisent la maison.
Builders are building the house.

_____

b. Le conducteur conduit le train.
The driver drives the train.

_____

c. La serveuse sert le repas.
The waitress is serving the meal.

_____

d. Le père lit un livre à ses enfants.
The father is reading a book to his children.

_____

e. Tout le monde connaît cette actrice.
Everybody knows this actress.

_____

f. Quelqu'un lave les fenêtres.
Someone is cleaning the windows.

_____

g. Les usines produisent des parfums.
Factories make perfumes.

_____

EXPRESSING POSSIBILITIES
LES HYPOTHÈSES

To express possibilities in French, you have different options, depending on the likelihood of the possibilities. A conditional sentence is made of two parts or clauses, the condition part introduced by "**si**" (*if*) and the result part that is dependent on the condition part to be met.

For example:

    a. Si tu viens, nous irons nous promener.
       If you come, we'll go for a walk.

    b. Si tu pars maintenant, tu auras ton train.
       If you go now, you'll catch your train.

There are three main levels of likelihood that will be useful to you: Very likely, likely, unlikely. What changes among these sentences are the tenses you use. For something that is <u>very likely</u>:

Si + subject + present tense..., subject + present tense...

    a. Si tu **parles** fort, tout le monde **entend**.
       If you speak loudly, everyone can hear it

For a possibility that is <u>likely</u>:

Si + subject + present tense..., subject + future tense...

    a. Si les enfants se **couchent** tard, ils **seront** fatigués demain.
       If the kids go to bed late, they will be tired tomorrow.

Finally, for a possibility that is <u>unlikely</u>:

Si + subject + imperfect tense..., subject + conditional...

    a. Si je gagnais au loto, j'emmènerais toute la famille faire un tour du monde.
       If I won the lottery, I would take the whole family on a world tour.

EXERCISES
EXERCICES

1. **Read the sentences and indicate the level of likelihood used: very likely, likely, unlikely**. *Lisez les phrases puis indiquez le niveau de probabilité donné : très probable, probable, peu probable.*

   a. Si tu crois que c'est vrai, tu te trompes.
   If you believe it's true, you're wrong. _____

   b. Si vous m'appelez dimanche, je ne répondrai pas.
   If you call me on Sunday, I won't answer. _____

   c. Si vous aviez une voiture pour les vacances, vous partiriez en voyage.
   If you had a car for the holidays, you'd go on a trip. _____

   d. Si vous aimez la cuisine française, je vous recommande le bistrot du coin.
   If you like French cuisine, I recommend the bistro on the corner of the street. _____

   e. Si vous deviez changer de métier, qu'est-ce que vous choisiriez ?
   If you had to change jobs, what would you choose? _____

LOGICAL RELATIONS
LES RELATIONS LOGIQUES

Logical relations are expressed by **linking words** that indicate the type of link there is between two parts of a sentence. The ones we are going to focus on can express **a cause, a consequence, a goal, an opposition, or a concession**. Those will be helpful to you in most situations.

Linking words for causes:

- **parce que** / because,

- **car** / because,

- **à cause de** + **nom** / because of (negative),

- **grâce à** + **nom** / thanks to

  a. Nous étions en retard **parce que** Mathis ne s'est pas levé.
     We were late because Mathis didn't wake up.

  b. Ils ont gagné **grâce à** Anaïs.
     They won thanks to Anaïs. (Positive cause)

  c. Vous avez perdu **car** vous n'étiez pas concentrés.
     You lost because you weren't focused.

Linking words for consequences:

- **donc** / so,

- **c'est pourquoi** / that's why,

- **alors** / so

  a. Il pleuvait **donc** nous ne sommes pas sortis.
     It was raining so we didn't go out.

  b. Paula voulait arriver tôt **c'est pourquoi** nous avons pris la voiture.
     Paula wanted to arrive early; that's why we took the car.

Linking words to express a goal are followed by an infinitive verb:

- **pour** / to,

- **afin de** / in order to,

- **dans le but de** / so as to

    a. Il a travaillé dur **pour** réussir son examen.
    He worked hard to pass his exam.

    b. Ils ont appelé les voisins **dans le but** d'avoir des explications.
    They called the neighbors so as to get an explanation.

Linking words of opposition:

- **mais** / but,

- **par contre** / however,

- **en revanche** / on the other hand,

- **cependant** / yet,

- **malgré le fait que** / despite the fact that

    a. Je n'ai pas vu ta sœur **par contre** j'ai vu ton frère.
    I haven't seen your sister, however I saw your brother.

    b. Tu ne peux pas m'aider **en revanche** tu peux m'accompagner.
    You can't help me, on the other hand, you can come with me.

Linking words of concession:

- **alors que** / even though,

- **même si** / even if

    a. Même si nous n'avons pas vu tout le château, nous avons vu beaucoup de choses.
    Even if we didn't see the whole castle, we saw a lot of things.

    b. Il a étudié toute la nuit alors que l'examen était reporté.
    He studied all night even though the exam was postponed.

EXERCISES
EXERCICES

1. Complete the sentences with the right linking word. *Complétez la phrase avec le bon mot de liaison.*

a. Il n'est pas venu _____ il est malade.
He didn't come because he is sick.

b. Les taxis sont chers à Paris _____ le métro n'est pas cher.
Taxis are expensive in Paris; on the other hand, the subway is cheap.

c. _____ je ne suis pas d'accord, je viendrais avec toi.
Even if I don't agree, I'll go with you.

d. Elle a répété au piano toute la semaine _____ réussir son audition.
She rehearsed on the piano all week so as to pass her audition.

e. Le restaurant avait oublié leur réservation _____ elles sont parties.
The restaurant had forgotten their reservation, that's why they left.

CONCLUSION

CONCLUSION

Félicitations ! *Congratulations!* You have reached the end of this workbook on French grammar and that is no small feat! French is known for having a complicated grammar, but nothing is too complicated when you take the time to understand it. You managed to learn a lot with this book and that will help you a lot in your progress. We hope you enjoyed those activities and that you are motivated to continue your learning journey through the French language.

When you learn a new language, it can be a bit frustrating because what comes to you in a flash in your native language requires time and thinking in that new language. But remember that's how you started when you were little and learning your own native language. The key to success is to be patient and to keep at it. To help you stay motivated, try to find a very specific reason why you want to learn French, like going on a trip to France in a few months or your company is developing a new branch with French people. With this specific reason, set yourself a very specific timeline. It will help you to remain consistent.

Also, you need to practice this new language as much as possible and you need to surround yourself with this new language you're learning. Thanks to the internet, there are many ways to do so:

- Reading: you can download the app of French newspapers, for example. Even if you don't understand everything, the headlines will give you some easy reading practice every day, especially if you turn on notifications. Written French will come to you. If you use social media, you can start following French people on Twitter or Instagram to have daily French content.

- Listening and Reading: you can watch French movies and French TV shows thanks to streaming services. To start, you can use the English subtitles to follow the plot. You will be hearing French and getting used to the pronunciation and the accents and that's already a good start! After a while, you can try to watch a short episode you've already seen but only with French subtitles. It will be a challenge but that's the best way to learn!

- Listening and Pronunciation: you can listen to French songs! Whatever your preferred genre is, you can find songs on YouTube or streaming services. You can find the lyrics and read them as you listen to the song. You can also practice your pronunciation by singing along.

- Speaking and Writing: this is the most challenging one because you need to find a French person to speak with you but also because it is the hardest skill with writing. It is much easier to listen and read, it's rather passive and you can play or read it again, but conversation doesn't give you much time. You could try to find a pen pal to get started. It is a bit easier with writing, you have a bit more time to think about what you're trying to say and then later you can move on to simple spoken conversations.

There is only one way to improve and it's through practice! Set up a few daily or weekly habits that will allow you to practice French without too much effort. French is a beautiful language and there is still a lot more you can learn, so don't hesitate to check out the other books written in this collection. **À très bientôt !** *See you soon!*

ANSWER KEY
RÉPONSES AUX EXERCICES

Le verbe être. *The verb to be*

1) **a)** viennent
   b) Je, suis
   c) es
   d) Je, Je suis
   e) êtes, Nous, sommes

   f) est, est
   g) es
   h) suis
   i) vous êtes
   j) nous sommes

2) **a)** Je suis marié/mariée/célibataire
   b) Je suis scientifique/artiste
   c) Je suis parisienne/bordelaise
   d) Je suis d'Italie/du Vietnam
   e) Je suis de Malaysie/d'Argentine.

3) **b)** Je m'appelle Chiara. Je suis italienne. Je suis de Livourne. Je suis chez un ami à Pékin.
   c) Je m'appelle Hao Dong. Je suis chinois. Je suis de Dandong. Je suis à l'Hôtel Aspen à New York.
   d) Je m'appelle Viktoriya. Je suis bulgare. Je suis de Sofia. Je suis chez mes cousins à Oslo.
   e) Je m'appelle Paulo. Je suis brésilien. Je suis de Sao Paulo. Je suis dans ma maison de vacances à Marrakech.
   f) Je suis Steve. Je suis anglais. Je suis de Newcastle. Je suis au camping Les Hirondelles.

Adjectives. *Les adjectifs*

1) **a)** Madame Martin est sympathi**que**.
   b) Ma tante est intelligent**e**.
   c) Ma sœur est blond**e**.
   d) La fille est souriant**e**.
   e) Ma mère est créati**ve**.

2) **a)** jaloux
   b) bruns
   c) roses

   d) colorées
   e) originaux

3)
a) blonde et petite
b) blond et petit
c) gentil et professionnel
d) gentille et professionnelle
e) belle et sympathique
f) beau, sympathique
g) bronzé et musclé
h) bronzée et musclée

Negation and interrogation. *Négation et interrogation*

1)
a) La porte **n'**est **pas** fermée
b) Je **ne** suis **pas** du Pérou
c) La salade **n'**est **pas** bonne
d) Ils **n'**ont **pas** plusieurs ordinateurs
e) Ceci **n'**est **pas** un masque

2)
b) Moi non plus.
c) Moi non plus.
d) Moi aussi.
e) Moi non plus.
f) Moi aussi.

Nouns and articles. *Noms et articles*

1)
a) Une chatte noire
b) La chienne, grande
c) La chanteuse grecque, brune
d) Ma femme, forte, sympathique
e) une actrice française connue
f) La voisine chinoise, sympathique, créative

2)
a) Le, la
b) le, la
c) La, La
d) La
e) le

3)
a) Un
b) Un
c) Une
d) Une
e) Une
f) Un
g) Une
h) Un
i) Une
j) Un
k) Une

Singular and plural of nouns.

1) Ce matin, je me suis levé et j'ai bu **un café allongé (des cafés allongés)**. J'ai mangé **un croissant (des croissants), une fraise mûre (des fraises mûres)** et **une orange sanguine (des oranges sanguines)**. Ensuite, j'ai vu **un vélo (des vélos)** devant ma maison. Mon voisin a **une amie américaine (des amies américaines)**. D'habitude, ses amis américains lui ramènent **un ordinateur (des ordinateurs)** des États-Unis.

J'ai **un fils (des fils)** et **une fille (des filles)**. Je les ai emmenés à l'école à 8 h 30. Ils ont **un instituteur (des instituteurs)** et deux institutrices qui sont très sympathiques.

En cours de sport, le professeur a donné **une balle (des balles)** aux élèves. Ils se sont beaucoup amusés.

Le soir, **le chat (les chats)** du voisin est venu dans notre maison. Il joue avec **le chien (les chiens)** du voisin, parfois. Ils sont très mignons.

2)
   a) Des yeux verts
   b) Des cheveux marrons
   c) Des chats blancs
   d) Des animaux de compagnie
   e) Des bijoux magnifiques
   f) Des pneus crevés
   g) Des chevaux merveilleux

Articles.

1) Je regarde **un** film à **la** télévision. Il y a **un** scientifique qui rencontre **un** investisseur. Ils décident de signer **un** contrat ensemble pour cloner **des** dinosaures et d'autres animaux qui ont disparu. Ensuite, le scientifique et ses deux enfants sont sur **une** île magnifique. **Les** oiseaux de l'île sont magnifiques et colorés. **Le** film est très intéressant. Mon frère n'a que huit ans et **les** dinosaures lui font peur donc il arrête de regarder quand **les** premiers dinosaures apparaissent.

Pendant **le** film, **des** amis de mes parents arrivent et nous regardons **la** télévision ensemble. **L'**amie de ma mère n'aime pas **le** café donc elle boit du thé. Mon père boit **un** verre de lait.

Après **le** film, nous allons marcher en forêt. Nous ne marchons qu'une heure, car c'est bientôt **la** nuit. **Une** voiture et **un** tracteur passent devant nous. Ce sont des amis du village. **La** nuit tombe donc nous devons rentrer à **la** maison. Bonne nuit.

« C'est » et « ce sont »

1)
    a) Ce sont
    b) Ce sont
    c) c'est
    d) C'est
    e) C'est
    f) C'est
    g) c'est
    h) Ce sont

    i) Ce sont
    j) ce sont
    k) C'est
    l) c'est
    m) Ce sont
    n) C'est
    o) C'est

2)
    a) C'est Albert Einstein.
    b) C'est ma cousine Lili.
    c) Mon voisin.
    d) Ce sont mes parents. / C'est ma maman et mon papa.
    e) C'est mon professeur de mathématiques.

Possessives. *Les possessifs*

1)
    a) mon
    b) leurs
    c) leurs, leurs
    d) son

    e) votre
    f) ton
    g) son
    h) leur

2)
    a) C'est le mien
    b) Ce sont les siens
    c) C'est la vôtre
    d) C'est le sien

    e) Ce sont les leurs
    f) Ce sont les siennes
    g) C'est la leur
    h) C'est le sien

Les noms de parentés et de groupe. *Nouns related to relatives and sense of belonging*

1)
    a) leur petit-fils
    b) sa grand-mère
    c) sa mère
    d) sa femme

    e) leur fils
    f) leur belle-fille
    g) leur beau-fils

2) Sophie est ma mère. Luc est mon père. Claire est ma sœur. Paul est mon frère. Julien est mon oncle. Élise est ma tante. Marie est ma cousine. Thomas est mon cousin. Anna est ma grand-mère. Henri est mon grand-père.

Sophie is my mother. Luc is my father. Claire is my sister. Paul is my brother. Julien is my uncle. Élise is my aunt. Marie is my cousin. Thomas is my cousin. Anna is my grandmother. Henri is my grandfather.

Demonstratives. *Les démonstratifs*

1)
  a) Ce
  b) Cette
  c) Ces
  d) Ces
  e) Ces

  f) Cette
  g) Cette
  h) Cet
  i) Ce

2)
  a) celui
  b) celui
  c) celle

  d) celui
  e) ceux
  f) celle

« Il y a » and « c'est »

1)
  a) Il y a. Ce sont
  b) Il y a. C'est
  c) Il y a. C'est
  d) Il y a. C'est

Expressing locations. *Situer dans l'espace*

1)
  a. Le
  b. X
  c. La
  d. X

  e. X
  f. La
  g. Les
  h. Les

2)
  a) aux, en
  b) en, en
  c) en, en

  d) en, en
  e) en, en
  f) aux, au, en

Numbers. *Les nombres*

1)
  a) 06.22.35.90.41
  b) 4,1
  c) 276,98 €
  d) 466, 4 h 30

2) Premier – deuxième – troisième – quatrième – cinquième – sixième – septième – huitième – neuvième – dixième

Le temps. *The weather*

1) **a)** Nous sommes le quinze décembre deux milles vingt-deux.

b) Nous sommes le sept mars mille neuf cent deux.

c) Nous sommes le neuf août mille neuf cent soixante-douze.

2) Il est une heure et quart. 1.15 AM

Il est treize heures et quart. 1.15 PM

Il est sept heures et quart. 7.15 AM

Il est dix-neuf heures et quart. 7.15 PM

Il est une heure moins le quart / Il est minuit quarante-cinq. 12.45 AM

Il est une heure moins le quart / Il est midi quarante-cinq. 12.45 PM

3) **a.** Il y a du brouillard

b. C'est nuageux

c. C'est pluvieux

d. C'est orageux

e. C'est ensoleillé

f. C'est venteux

g. C'est neigeux

Indefinites. *Les indéfinis*

1) **a)** Chaque

b) aucune

c) quelques

d) plusieurs

e) Certaines

f) tous

Duration. *La durée*

1) **a)** depuis

b) pour

c) pendant

d) depuis

e) il y a

f) pendant

g) pour

h) depuis

i) il y a

Adverbs. *Les adverbes*

1)
  a) rapidement
  b) fortement
  c) heureusement
  d) certainement

  e) constamment
  f) silencieusement
  g) évidemment

2)
  a) rarement
  b) prudemment
  c) silencieusement
  d) bien

  e) mieux
  f) facilement
  g) franchement

Expressing quantities. *Les quantités*

1)
  a) du, des, de la
  b) quatre, une, un
  c) beaucoup de
  d) trop de

  e) du, de la
  f) de, un, des
  g) assez de

The pronoun « en ». *Le pronom « en »*

1)
  a) J'en ai deux.
  b) Oui, j'en mange.
  c) Oui, il y en a.
  d) Oui, il en a parlé.

  e) Il y en a trois.
  f) Oui, j'en ai trouvé.
  g) Oui, j'en veux une.
  h) Oui, il en reste.

Comparative and Superlative. *Comparatif et superlatif*

1)
  a) plus petite que
  b) moins attentivement que
  c) aussi long que

  d) meilleur que
  e) moins de temps que
  f) convient autant que

2)
  a) le moins beau
  b) le plus mauvais vin que
  c) le mieux
  d) le moins rapidement
  e) éclaire le plus
  f) le plus d'énergie

The verb to go. *Le verbe aller*

1) **a)** vais chez
   b) vas demander à
   c) va chez
   d) allons parler de
   e) allez aimer
   f) vont à

2) **a)** Je **vais** à la piscine.
   b) Thomas **va étudier** le droit.
   c) Les enfants **vont voir** un film samedi soir.
   d) Le president **va faire** un discours.
   e) Je **vais inviter** tout le monde au restaurant.

The pronoun « y ». *Le pronom y*

1) **a)** Le chat **y** dort toute la journée.
   b) Paul adore **y** jouer.
   c) Lucile **y** est.
   d) Cédric pense à **y** déménager.

2) **a)** Oui, nous **y** allons.
   b) Oui, elle **y** pense.
   c) Oui, j'**y** vais.
   d) Oui, nous **y** réfléchissons.

Les pronoms compléments. *Complement pronouns*

1) **a)** Je l'invite à dîner.
   b) Nous **les** présentons à nos amis.
   c) Je **te** montre mon salon demain.
   d) Tu **le lui** as dit ?
   e) Elles **m'**ont téléphoné pour **m'en** parler.

2) **a)** Je l'aime beaucoup.
   b) Je **lui** ai parlé.
   c) Il **leur** appartient.
   d) Oui, ils **m'**ont croisé.

Stressed or disjunctive pronouns. *Les pronoms toniques*

1) **a)** toi

  b) moi

  c) elle, lui

  d) Elle

  e) eux

  f) vous, elles

Relative pronouns. *Les relatives*

1) **a)** que

  b) qui

  c) que

  d) dont

  e) où

  f) à qui

2) **a)** C'est un arbre **qui** est grand et **qui** est vert.

  b) Voici une maison **que** je veux acheter et **qui** me plaît.

  c) J'ai déménagé en 2018 **quand** j'étais fleuriste.

  d) J'ai croisé un voisin **qui** m'a parlé du barbecue de la semaine prochaine **dont** je ne me souvenais pas.

  e) C'est une salle de sport **où** je vais tous les vendredis **qui** est un peu chère.

Interrogation. *Interrogation*

1) **a)** Comment s'appelle-t-il ?

  b) Où vont-ils ?

  c) Que faites-vous ici ?

  d) Comment est-ce que tu vas au travail

  e) À quoi penses-tu ?

Negation – advanced. *Négation – advanced*

1) La famille Dupont **ne** vit **pas** dans une grande maison. Ils **n'**ont **pas de** chien **ni de** chat. Il **n'**y a **pas d'**enfants. L'aîné, Victor, **ne** vit **plus** chez ses parents pendant ses études. La cadette, Laura, **n'**aime **pas** jouer au football. Constance, la mère, travaille **sans** son ordinateur à la maison. Léni, le père, **ne** passe **pas** ses journées au bureau. Il **n'**y va **ni** à vélo **ni** à pied.

Indirect speech in the present tense. *Le discours indirect au présent*

1) a) Lola demande pourquoi **nous** déménageons.
    b) Thomas dit **qu'**il y a beaucoup de boulangeries en France.
    c) Les Français **disent** qu'**ils** ne mangent pas trop de pain.
    d) Les Françaises disent **qu'elles** aiment marcher.

2) a) Amélia me demande si je vais m'asseoir à côté d'elle.
    b) Les enfants **disent qu'ils ne veulent** pas aller **se** coucher.
    c) Timothé **demande si nous allons** souvent à la salle de sport.
    d) **Je te demande si** tu vas à Paris la semaine prochaine.
    e) **Tu dis que tu n'aimes** pas les tomates.

Prepositions. *Les prépositions*

1) 2) Le chat est devant le mur.
    3) Le chat est sur le coussin/canapé.
    4) Le chat est devant le canapé.
    5) Le chat est derrière le canapé.
    6) Le chat est à côté du canapé.
    7) Le poisson est dans l'aquarium.
    8) Le chat est dans l'aquarium.
    9) Le chien est sous la table basse.
    10) La souris est entre le chat et le chien**.**

2) a) à
    b) du
    c) vers
    d) en
    e) à
    f) pendant

The passive voice. *Le passif*

1) **a)** La maison **est construite** par les ouvriers.
   b) Le train **est conduit** par le conducteur.
   c) Le repas **est servi** par la serveuse.
   d) Le livre **est lu** aux enfants (par leur père).
   e) Cette actrice **est connue** (de tous).
   f) Les fenêtres **sont lavées** (par quelqu'un).
   g) Les parfums **sont produits** par des usines.

Expressing possibilities. *Les hypothèses*

1) **a)** Very likely
   b) Likely
   c) Unlikely.
   d) Very likely.
   e) Unlikely.

Logical relations. *Les relations logiques*

2) **a)** parce qu'
   b) en revanche
   c) Même si
   d) afin de
   e) c'est pourquoi

MORE BOOKS BY LINGO MASTERY

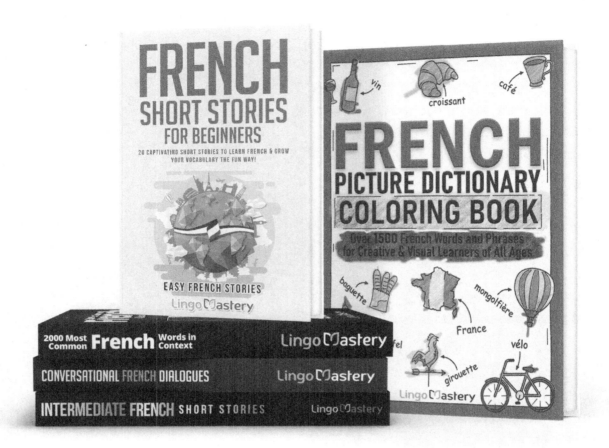

We are not done teaching you French until you're fluent!

Here are some other titles you might find useful in your journey of mastering French:

✓ French Short Stories for Beginners

✓ Intermediate French Short Stories

✓ 2000 Most Common French Words in Context

✓ Conversational French Dialogues

But we got many more!

Check out all of our titles at **www.lingomastery.com/french**

Printed in Great Britain
by Amazon

48513873R00110